GOODWILL'S

SELF HELP TO ENGLISH CONVERSATION

Revised Edition

REKHA CHANDRA

Edited By

MADAN SOOD

GOODWILL PUBLISHING HOUSE®
B-3 RATTAN JYOTI, 18 RAJENDRA PLACE
NEW DELHI-110008 (INDIA)

Published by:

GOODWILL PUBLISHING HOUSE®

B-3 Rattan Jyoti, 18 Rajendra Place
New Delhi–110008 (INDIA)
Phones: 25820556, 25750801
Fax: 91-11-25764396
E-mail: goodwillpub@vsnl.net
ylp@bol.net.in
Website: goodwillpublishinghouse.com

Printed at : Kumar Offset Printers, Delhi-110092

Contents

Introduction

English is spoken in many parts of the world, *i.e.* Britain, America, South Africa, Australia, New Zealand, Canada, India, etc. English learners look to British English as the centre of an English speaking world.

Conversation is an informal exchange of ideas through spoken words. When we converse, we engage ourselves in conversation about various subjects. Language is the method of human communication, either spoken or written, consisting of the use of words in an agreed way.

The aim of this book is to turn the learner into a conversationist—one who is good at or is fond of conversing. Emphasis in this book is on the faculty of speech, style, expression and the use of words or specialized vocabulary. To speak is the act of an instance of uttering words, capable of articulate speech. An endeavour has been made to achieve this objective through step-by-step approach in the simplest possible way.

About this Book

This book will help you to learn on your own and achieve the following results:

1. Gain confidence to use the language effectively in everyday life.
2. Convey and receive messages on telephone.
3. Frame questions and respond to questions.
4. Express and report your personal opinions and feelings.
5. Participate confidently in familiar social situations.
6. Narrate incidents and events, real or imaginary, in a logical sequence.
7. Convey your ideas appropriately according to the requirement of audience, topic or purpose.
8. Speak intelligently with the help of sentence stress, word-stress, and intonation patterns.
9. Use pauses to make the meaning clear.
10. Become capable of speaking this foreign language with ease.

Practical Tips to Master English

Through my personal experience, I'd like to share a few tips with you, which will help you achieve your goal as fast as possible.

1. Get over your shyness and hesitation. English is a foreign language, and it doesn't really matter if we make mistakes during the learning stage.
2. Use the language as often as you can. The more you speak, the faster you will learn.
3. Maintain a personal register to note down the difficult areas, as you proceed with the book. Revise and re-do them.
4. Listen to the English news and other English programmes. Listen to English audio cassettes and CDs, even if you feel that you don't understand much. This is a very important listening activity to improve your pronunciation.
5. Read an extract from a magazine or a newspaper, underline the difficult words, find the meanings, write those down in your register, and then read the extract once again. This will help you to improve your vocabulary.
6. Make dictionary your best friend. Whenever in doubt regarding a meaning or pronunciation, refer to your dictionary.

7. Read aloud a short story, then change the tense and read it aloud once again.
8. Take any item, keep it in front of you, *i.e.* a painting, decoration piece, pencil, book, etc. and speak out as much as you can about that item. Repeat this exercise after completing each lesson. You can measure your progress accordingly.
9. Divide your register into two sections—pronunciation and vocabulary. Continue writing all the new words and the words which you find difficult to pronounce under the proper heading. You can revise these off and on.
10. Read a passage or recite a poem and record it.
11. Participate in group discussions with your friends on the subjects of your choice.
12. Memorize a passage on any topic, and then either record it or speak in front of a mirror.

1

Alphabet

There are 26 letters in the English Alphabet: A, B, C, D, E, F, G, H, I, J, K, L, M, N, O, P, Q, R, S, T, U, V, W, X, Y, Z.

English alphabet is divided into—

5 Vowels: a, e, i, o, u

21 Consonants: b, c, d, f, g, h, j, k, l, m, n, p, q, r, s, t, v, w, x, y, z

A, AN, THE

AN is used before a word beginning with a vowel sound.

an apple

an egg

an ice cream

an orange

an umbrella

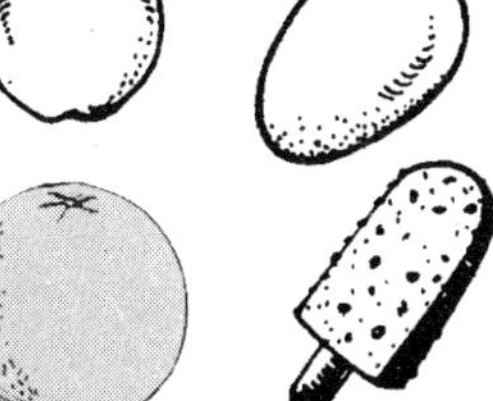

A is used before a word beginning with a consonant sound.

a ball

a cat

a doll

a fan

a girl

a house

a jug

a kite

a lamp

a map

a net

a pen

a queen

a rat

a snake

a table

a van

a watch

a xylophone

a yacht

a zoo

Note:

a university	a union
an hour	an heir

A is used before 'university' and 'union' because they give a consonant sound; on the other hand **AN** is used before 'hour' and 'heir' because they give a vowel sound.

> **THE** is used before singular and plural nouns and can be used before vowels and consonants.

The apple	The apples
The egg	The eggs
The ice cream	The ice creams
The orange	The oranges
The umbrella	The umbrellas
The ball	The balls
The cat	The cats
The doll	The dolls
The fan	The fans
The girl	The girls
The house	The houses
The jug	The jugs
The kite	The kites
The lamp	The lamps
The map	The maps
The net	The nets
The pen	The pens
The queen	The queens
The rat	The rats
The snake	The snakes
The table	The tables
The van	The vans

The watch	The watches
The xylophone	The xylophones
The yacht	The yachts
The zoo	The zoos

THE is also used for some particular person or thing.

1. He tore the blue book.
2. The handle of that big jar is lying here.
3. The moon is looking beautiful.
4. The fat man was walking very slowly.
5. The ball in your hand belongs to me.

ASSIGNMENT

Read the lesson loudly.

Write down 26 different words with A, AN and THE.

EXERCISE 1

Make words with the following letters:

1. l l b a ____________

2. g b a ____________

3. a c t ____________

4. o l l d ____________

5. d g o ____________

6. e d b ____________

EXERCISE 2

Fill in the blanks with *A*, *AN* or *THE*.

1. He gave me __________ apple. __________ apple was delicious.
2. We have bought __________ new house. __________ house has five big rooms.
3. I met __________ angry man.
4. __________ honest man will not steal.
5. It was __________ hottest day of the year.
6. The boy asked __________ question.
7. The question asked by __________ boy was difficult.
8. I bought __________ umbrella yesterday. __________ umbrella was made of plastic.
9. __________ accident took place near our house.
10. He lost _______ eye in _______ accident. ______ accident took place last year.

SHAPES

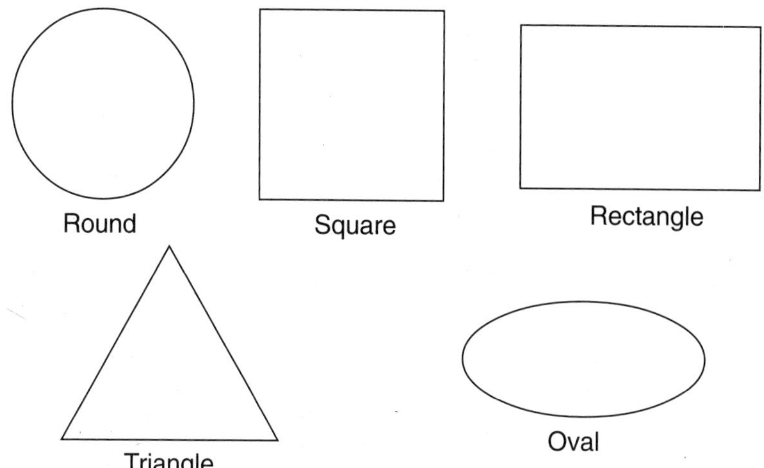

E.g.

1. This is a **round** table
2. A **square** has four equal sides.
3. This room is **rectangular**.
4. The blue kite is **triangular**.
5. An egg is **oval** in shape.

ASSIGNMENT

Make five sentences with the five shapes mentioned above.

CARDINAL AND ORDINAL NUMBERS

Cardinal Number		Ordinal Number	
words	*figures*		
One	1	First	1st
Two	2	Second	2nd
Three	3	Third	3rd
Four	4	Fourth	4th
Five	5	Fifth	5th
Six	6	Sixth	6th
Seven	7	Seventh	7th
Eight	8	Eighth	8th
Nine	9	Ninth	9th
Ten	10	Tenth	10th
Eleven	11	Eleventh	11th
Twelve	12	Twelfth	12th
Thirteen	13	Thirteenth	13th
Fourteen	14	Fourteenth	14th
Fifteen	15	Fifteenth	15th
Sixteen	16	Sixteenth	16th

Seventeen	17	Seventeenth	17th
Eighteen	18	Eighteenth	18th
Nineteen	19	Nineteenth	19th
Twenty	20	Twentieth	20th
Thirty	30	Thirtieth	30th
Forty	40	Fortieth	40th
Fifty	50	Fiftieth	50th (half-century)
Sixty	60	Sixtieth	60th
Seventy	70	Seventieth	70th
Eighty	80	Eightieth	80th
Ninety	90	Ninetieth	90th
One hundred	100	One hundredth	100th (century)
One thousand	1000		
Twenty-one	21	Twenty-first	21st
Twenty-two	22	Twenty-second	22nd
Twenty-three	23	Twenty-third	23rd
Twenty-four	24	Twenty-fourth	24th
Twenty-five	25	Twenty-fifth	25th
Twenty-six	26	Twenty-sixth	26th
Twenty-seven	27	Twenty-seventh	27th
Twenty-eight	28	Twenty-eighth	28th
Twenty-nine	29	Twenty-ninth	29th
Thirty-one	31	Thirty-first	31st
Thirty-two	32	Thirty-second	32nd
Thirty-three	33	Thirty-third	33rd
Thirty-four	34	Thirty-fourth	34th
Thirty-five	35	Thirty-fifth	35th

Thirty-six	36	Thirty-sixth	36th
Thirty-seven	37	Thirty-seventh	37th
Thirty-eight	38	thirty-eighth	38th
Thirty-nine	39	thirty-ninth	39th
Forty-one	41	forty-first	41st
Forty-two	42	forty-second	42nd
Forty-three	43	forty-third	43rd
Forty-four	44	forty-fourth	44th
Forty-five	45	forty-fifth	45th
Forty-six	46	forty-sixth	46th
Forty-seven	47	forty-seventh	47th
Forty-eight	48	forty-eighth	48th
Forty-nine	49	forty-ninth	49th

Examples:

1. What is the date?
   It's May, the twenty-sixth.
   It's the twenty-sixth of May.
2. When's your birthday?
   My birthday is on November, the twenty-fifth.
   It's on twenty-fifth of November.
3. What time is it?
   It's 8.30 a.m.
4. What day is it?
   It is Monday.
5. What's the date?
   It's the sixteenth of August.
6. What's the weather like?
   It's raining.

2

This, That, These, Those, Is, Are

THIS, THAT, THESE AND THOSE

This and **that** are used with singular words.

These and **those** are used with plural words.

This and **these** are used for things which are close to us.

That and **those** are used for things which are far away from us.

Singular (close by)	**Plural (close by)**
This apple	These apples
This egg	These eggs
This ice cream	These ice creams
This orange	These oranges
This umbrella	These umbrellas
This ball	These balls
This cat	These cats
This doll	These dolls
This fan	These fans
This girl	These girls

This house	These houses
This jug	These jugs
This kite	These kites
This lamp	These lamps
This map	These maps
This net	These nets
This pen	These pens
This queen	These queens
This rat	These rats
This snake	These snakes
This table	These tables
This van	These vans
This watch	These watches
This xylophone	These xylophones
This yacht	These yachts
This zoo	These zoos

Singular (far away)	**Plural (far away)**
That apple	Those apples
That egg	Those eggs
That ice cream	Those ice creams
That orange	Those oranges
That umbrella	Those umbrellas
That ball	Those balls
That cat	Those cats
That doll	Those dolls
That fan	Those fans
That girl	Those girls

That house	Those houses
That jug	Those jugs
That kite	Those kites
That lamp	Those lamps
That map	Those maps
That net	Those nets
That pen	Those pens
That queen	Those queens
That rat	Those rats
That snake	Those snakes
That table	Those tables
That van	Those vans
That watch	Those watches
That xylophone	Those xylophones
That yacht	Those yachts
That zoo	Those zoos

PRACTICAL ASSIGNMENT

Keep a number of articles close to you and practise the use of 'this' and 'these'. After that put all the articles far away from you and practise the use of 'that' and 'those'.

OPPOSITES

fat	thin
big	small
tall	short
high	low
clean	dirty

beautiful	ugly
bad	good
heavy	light
hard	soft
early	late

EXERCISE 3

Fill in the blanks with opposites.

1. John is fat, but Joe is ______________.
2. Mary is ______________, but Jane is short.
3. Her bag is big, but his bag is ______________.
4. This chair is ______________, but that chair is low.
5. Edward's house is ______________, but Mary's house is dirty.
6. Sarah is beautiful, but her sister is ______________.
7. Tom is a ______________ boy, but his friend is a bad boy.
8. This box is heavy, but that box is ______________.
9. The white toy is soft, but the brown toy ______________.
10. Ted gets up early, but David gets up ______________.

ASSIGNMENT

Make ten sentences on your own, and read them aloud.

IS AND ARE

Is is used with this and that.

Are is used with these and those.

This is an apple.	These are apples.
That is an apple.	Those are apples.
This is an egg.	These are eggs.
That is an egg.	Those are eggs.
This is an ice cream.	These are ice creams.
That is an ice cream.	Those are ice creams.
This is an orange.	These are oranges.
That is an orange.	Those are oranges.
This is an umbrella.	These are umbrellas.
That is an umbrella.	Those are umbrellas.
This is a ball.	These are balls.
That is a ball	Those are balls.
This is a cat.	These are cats.
That is a cat.	Those are cats.
This is a doll.	These are dolls.
That is a doll.	Those are dolls.
This is a fan.	These are fans.
That is a fan.	Those are fans.
This is a girl.	These are girls.
That is a girl.	Those are girls.
This is a house.	These are houses.
That is a house.	Those are houses.
This is a jug.	These are jugs.
That is a jug.	Those are jugs.
This is a kite.	These are kites.
That is a kite.	Those are kites.
This is a lamp.	These are lamps.
That is a lamp.	Those are lamps.
This is a map.	These are maps.

That is a map.
This is a net.
That is a net.
This is a pen.
That is a pen.
This is a queen.
That is a queen.
This is a rat.
That is a rat.
This is a snake.
That is a snake.
This is a table.
That is a table.
This is a van.
That is a van.
This is a watch.
That is a watch.
This is a xylophone.
That is a xylophone.
This is a yacht.
That is a yacht.
This is a zoo.
That is a zoo.

Those are maps.
These are nets.
Those are nets.
These are pens.
Those are pens.
These are queens.
Those are queens.
These are rats.
Those are rats.
These are snakes.
Those are snakes.
These are tables.
Those are tables.
These are vans.
Those are vans.
These are watches.
Those are watches.
These are xylophones.
Those are xylophones.
These are yachts.
These are yachts.
These are zoos.
Those are zoos.

ASSIGNMENT

Read aloud all the above sentences.

Make your own sentences like the ones shown above, using the following words:

bat, glass, pencil, boy, chair, bed, shirt, curtain, tin, banana, hand, pot, plate, rubber, painting, igloo, engine, animal, art, nest.

COLOURS

Red	apple
Yellow	lemon
Green	leaf
Pink	rose
White	milk
Blue	sky
Orange	orange (fruit)
Purple	eggplant (brinjal)
Brown	log
Black	shoe

This shirt is red.

That shirt is blue.

This bus is yellow.

That bus is green.

This car is white.

That car is brown.

This pen is black.

That pen is pink.

This pencil is purple.

That pencil is orange.

EXERCISE 4

Fill in the blanks with appropriate colours:

1. This flower is ___________.
2. Those flowers are ___________.
3. That tree is ___________.
4. These trees are ___________.
5. This cap is ___________.
6. Those caps are ___________.
7. That ball is ___________.
8. These balls are ___________.
9. This kite is ___________.
10. Those kites are ___________.

ASSIGNMENT

Make ten sentences on your own with the colours you know. Read the sentences aloud.

3

Sentences, Kinds of Sentences, Practice Sentences

SENTENCES

1. A **sentence** is a group of words that makes complete sense.
2. The words in a sentence must be placed in their proper order to make complete sense.
3. A sentence begins with a capital letter and ends with a full stop (.) or a question mark (?) or an exclamation mark (!).
4. A sentence may be made up of just one word, but that word can only be a verb, *e.g.* walk, jump, sleep, run, stop, etc.
5. A sentence has a **subject** and a **predicate**.
   (a) The part of the sentence which names what the sentence is about is the **subject**.
   (b) That part of the sentence which says something about the subject is the **predicate.**

EXERCISE 5

Column A gives a list of subjects and column B gives a list of predicates. Match the subjects with their predicates. Write the number of the subject against the correct predicate. The first five have been done for you.

Subject Column A		**Predicate** Column B
1. My drawing	3	was very serious.
2. The prisoner		ended in a draw.
3. The accident		is ill.
4. Only bright students	1	was praised by everyone.
5. Every Indian		drives very fast.
6. Two matches	2	escaped from the jail.
7. My grandmother	5	is proud of India.
8. The driver	4	secure good marks.
9. The doctor		is eating an ice cream.
10. The fat girl		is seeing the patients.

EXERCISE 6

Supply the subjects for the following sentences:

1. ____________ gives us heat and light.

2. ____________ runs very fast.

3. ____________ sells medicines.

4. ____________ makes furniture.

5. ____________ has seven colours.

6. ____________ it is very cold.

7. ____________ is a faithful animal.

8. ____________ is a beautiful hill station.

9. ____________ is the capital of India.

10. ____________ looks after the house.

EXERCISE 7

Supply the predicates for the following sentences:

1. The car ____________________.
2. This man ____________________.
3. Many people ____________________.
4. A morning walk ____________________.
5. The doctor ____________________.
6. The wind ____________________.
7. The lion ____________________.
8. Rain ____________________.
9. The boys ____________________.
10. The river ____________________.

EXERCISE 8

Underline the predicates in the following sentences. The first one has been done for you.

1. Ramesh lives in Mumbai.
2. My mother cooks for me.
3. The birds build nests on trees.
4. Monkeys have long tails.
5. Harry is hitting the ball.
6. Anita lives near my house.
7. Joy jogs every day.
8. Bears like to eat honey.
9. My father is very strict.
10. The house is full of guests.

Read the following sentences carefully:

1. This door is made of wood.
2. I am sitting on a chair.
3. The items in the room have been placed beautifully.
4. I am an energetic boy.
5. Mohit is a naughty boy.
6. We cannot live without oxygen.
7. The branches of this tree are brown.
8. I am scratching the table.
9. My pencil box is very big.
10. The leaves are green.
11. My pencil is blunt.
12. I am wearing white shoes.
13. The sky is blue.
14. The curtain is too long.
15. There is a balcony in my house.
16. My school is very big.
17. There is a pen in my pencil box.
18. Children are playing in the park.
19. There are many trees in the park.
20. I live in Delhi.

ASSIGNMENT

Make sentences using the following words:

man, hand, air, bus, window, rain, train, aeroplane, inkpot, child, hospital, mother, parents, road, market, car, picnic, paper, blanket, servant.

Begin all the sentences with a capital letter and end them with a full stop.

REARRANGEMENT OF WORDS

The following words have been rearranged to make complete sense:

1. everywhere is air
   Air is everywhere.
2. with are fighting why him you
   Why are you fighting with him?
3. dark not do in play the
   Do not play in the dark.
4. snowed it yesterday heavily Srinagar in
   It snowed heavily in Srinagar yesterday.
5. Maya French speak can very well
   Maya can speak French very well.
6. home mother is your at
   Is your mother at home?
7. school is at someone there
   Is there someone at school?
8. you why he did call mad
   Why did he call you mad?
9. creams list a all make of these
   Make a list of all these creams.
10. annoy me not do
    Do not annoy me.
11. am unhappy very I
    I am very unhappy.
12. love you me do
    Do you love me?
13. intelligent are children his very
    His children are very intelligent.
14. month married next will he be
    He will be married next month.

15. some live in animals zoos
    Some animals live in zoos.
16. air travels only he by
    He travels only by air.
17. keeps she very house her well
    She keeps her house very well.
18. is good a she very cook
    She is a very good cook.
19. fine neighbour my is a lady
    My neighbour is a fine lady.
20. colourful birds are some very
    Some birds are very colourful.

EXERCISE 9

Rearrange the following words to make complete sense:

1. is white rubber this a

2. write I pencil with a

3. very this is chair high

4. in my there flowers are many garden

5. blanket have I brown a

6. on iron is table the the

7. dressing table window near is the the

8. are five there in room the chairs

9. pen a write I with

10. loudly is baby the crying

11. heavily raining outside is it

12. strict is teacher my very

13. sun boys are the in playing the

14. want ice cream I to eat

15. eat vegetables fresh like I to

16. garden full flowers of is the

17. small my is house

18. playing are the park children in

19. near there cement factory a is house my

20. box full clothes of the is

Affirmative and Negative Sentences

1. Sentences that make positive statements are called **affirmative sentences.**
2. Sentences that make negative statements are called **negative sentences.**

Affirmative	**Negative**
I am well.	I am not well.
Ravi was present.	Ravi was not present.
Girls are playing.	Girls are not playing.
They have eaten.	They have not eaten.
Boys are working.	Boys are not working.

Rules to convert affirmative sentences into negative sentences

1. We put **not** after the first verb to make the sentence negative if the verb is made up of two or more words, *e.g.*

   Affirmative

   (a) This girl can read well.

   (b) I shall take him home.

   (c) My uncle will give me money.

(d) You may have another banana.

(e) She must go there.

(f) You ought to help the poor.

Negative

(a) This girl cannot read well.

(b) I shall not take him home.

(c) My uncle will not give me money.

(d) You may not have another banana.

(e) She must not go there.

(f) You ought not to help the poor.

2. **Not** is used in the following sentences to make the verbs negative.

These verbs are: be, is, am, are, was, were, have, has, had, can, could, shall, should, will, would, may, might, must, ought.

Affirmative

(a) I am going away.

(b) They are running.

(c) The girls were playing.

(d) Jone has learnt his poem.

(e) He has caught the train.

(f) The thief was caught.

(g) The radio has been repaired.

Negative

(a) I am not going away.

(b) They are not running.

(c) The girls were not playing.

(d) Jone has not learnt his poem.

(e) He has not caught the train.

(f) The thief was not caught.

(g) The radio has not been repaired.

3. The following sentences change into the negative by putting **do not** before the verb:

(a) While speaking, we generally say don't instead of do not.

(b) After a negative in a sentence, *some* is changed to *any*.

Affirmative

(a) I speak English.

(b) We like chocolates.

(c) These girls sing well.

(d) Come in.

(e) Shut the window.

(f) Give her some food.

Negative

(a) I do not speak English.

(b) We do not like chocolates.

(c) These girls do not sing well.

(d) Do not come in.

(e) Do not shut the window.

(f) Do not give her any food.

4. In the following sentences, the third person singular of the present tense is changed into the negative form by placing **does not** before the first verb:

Affirmative

(a) Tony tells a lie.

(b) Rea speaks French.

(c) He writes well.

(d) She runs fast.

(e) Robert rides the bicycle.

(f) Mary climbs the stairs.

(g) Harry studies hard.

Negative

(a) Tony does not tell a lie.

(b) Rea does not speak French.

(c) He does not write well.

(d) She does not run fast.

(e) Robert does not ride the bicycle.

(f) Mary does not climb the stairs.

(g) Harry does not study hard.

5. The following sentences of the past tense change into the negative form by placing **did not** before the first verb:

Affirmative

(a) He lost his work.

(b) I met her two days back.

(c) The hare ran fast.

(d) Mona broke the window pane.

(e) He came home.

(f) They played for their school.

(g) Roma received a prize.

Negative

(a) He did not lose his book.

(b) I did not meet her two days back.

(c) The hare did not run fast.

(d) Mona did not break the window pane.

(e) He did not come home.

(f) They did not play for their school.

(g) Roma did not receive a prize.

EXERCISE 10

Change the following affirmative sentences into negative sentences:

1. She has a new frock.

____

2. We are friends.

____

3. You are the best swimmer.

____

4. They were absent today.

____

5. You may have a holiday tomorrow.

____

6. You look happy.

____

7. All of us like sweets.

____

8. Horses eat grass.

____

9. Put your pencils away.

____

10. Shut the door please.

____

11. She smiles at me.

____

12. It snows heavily in the mountains.

____

13. The sun shines brightly every day.

____

14. She drinks too much.

____

15. My uncle lives in London.

____

16. He slept before me.

____

17. I met a little school girl.

____

18. The dog ran after the cow.

____

19. The wolf killed the rabbit.

____

20. The lion roared loudly.

____

EXERCISE 11

Change the following negative sentences into affirmative sentences:

1. The ladies are not hungry.

   ____

2. The soldiers may not go.

   ____

3. The plants have not been watered.

   ____

4. Do not board a running bus.

   ____

5. John did not play well.

   ____

6. I do not know her.

   ____

7. Do not give him any water.

   ____

8. The man did not carry a heavy load.

   ____

9. We do not want to leave.

   ____

10. Do not read this magazine.

    ____

11. You should not always come alone.

    ____

12. She cannot solve this puzzle.

____

13. We do not go to church every day.

____

14. They do not pay for their drinks.

____

15. She does not sing well.

____

16. The water did not freeze in the bucket.

____

17. The cow does not give milk every day.

____

18. She did not go to school on her bicycle.

____

19. The old man did not shoot the deer.

____

20. The policeman did not catch the thief.

____

Kinds of Sentence

There are **four** kinds of sentences:

1. Assertive or declarative sentences
2. Interrogative or question sentences
3. Imperative sentences (command, request, advice)
4. Exclamatory sentences

1. A sentence that says or states something is called an **assertive** or **declarative sentence.**
    1. I go to office every day.
    2. He is an obedient boy.
    3. They will attend the conference.
    4. I have found my bag.
    5. His father is a lawyer.
    6. The baby is crying.
    7. I do not like this house.
    8. My sister is coming today.
    9. I love my father.
    10. The maid works very well.
    11. I am not feeling happy.
    12. I can swim.
    13. The shop is open.
    14. The dog is barking.
    15. That man is old.
    16. The child is running.
    17. I am driving the car.
    18. He sells chocolates.
    19. She is plucking flowers.
    20. She is teaching.
2. A sentence that asks a question is called an **interrogative** or **question sentence.**
    1. Who is coming to my house?
    2. Are you feeling thirsty?
    3. When will you go?
    4. What is his name?

5. Where does he work?
6. Do you go to school?
7. Are you happy?
8. Will you help me?
9. Will you cook for me?
10. Can you write?
11. Do you sing?
12. Do you swim?
13. When will you return?
14. How many books do you have?
15. How old are you?
16. Do you have a diary?
17. Do you have a big table?
18. Does he like ice creams?
19. What did he say?
20. How many dogs does he have?

3. A sentence that expresses a command, request or advice is called an **imperative sentence.**

   1. Be quiet.
   2. Do not talk.
   3. Finish your work.
   4. Eat it at once.
   5. Open the door.
   6. Close the gate.
   7. Do not go out.
   8. Call that boy.
   9. Do not climb that tree.

10. Give me this pen please.
11. Please give me a glass of milk.
12. Please sit down.
13. Listen to me.
14. Walk in a line please.
15. Form a queue please.
16. Please say something.
17. Wait for me for two minutes please.
18. Walk carefully.
19. Do not waste your time.
20. Listen to the instruction carefully.

4. A sentence that expresses a strong feeling is called an **exclamatory sentence**.

    1. How sunny the day is!
    2. How beautiful the rainbow is!
    3. How colourful this flower is!
    4. How picturesque this scenery is!
    5. What an amazing sight!
    6. What a splendid idea!
    7. What a silly mistake!
    8. What a question!
    9. What a choice!
    10. What a behaviour!
    11. What a temper!

12. How unfair!
13. What a thoughtless remark!
14. What a nuisance!
15. Hurrah! We have won.
16. Alas! She is dead.
17. Ah! It pains.
18. Wow! I like it.
19. Never heard of!
20. Hurrah! He has come.

EXERCISE 12

Mark the type of sentence—interrogative, assertive, imperative or exclamatory—in the following blanks:

1. How many books do you have? ____________
2. I have only one pencil. ____________
3. Show me your camera please. ____________
4. What a colourful dress! ____________
5. Can you bring one pen for me? ____________
6. Take this packet. ____________
7. Where is the parrot? ____________
8. The bird is in the cage. ____________
9. What a sweet voice! ____________
10. How ghastly was the accident! ____________
11. Do not bark, Brownie! ____________

12. Who teaches you French? ____________

13. I do not want to buy this. ____________

14. What is the time? ____________

15. Always speak loud. ____________

16. I missed the train. ____________

17. I am not going out. ____________

18. Have you taken your medicine? ____________

19. Please come to my office. ____________

20. Do not get angry. ____________

EXERCISE 13

Write a statement, a question and a command with each of the following words:

1. dog (statement) ____________

2. dog (question) ____________

3. dog (command) ____________

1. milk (statement) ____________

2. milk (question) ____________

3. milk (command) ____________

1. angry (statement) ____________

2. angry (question) ____________

3. angry (command) ____________

1.	bus	(statement)	________________
2.	bus	(question)	________________
3.	bus	(command)	________________
1.	pen	(statement)	________________
2.	pen	(question)	________________
3.	pen	(command)	________________
1.	house	(statement)	________________
2.	house	(question)	________________
3.	house	(command)	________________
1.	friend	(statement)	________________
2.	friend	(question)	________________
3.	friend	(command)	________________
1.	mother	(statement)	________________
2.	mother	(question)	________________
3.	mother	(command)	________________
1.	bird	(statement)	________________
2.	bird	(question)	________________
3.	bird	(command)	________________
1.	table	(statement)	________________
2.	table	(question)	________________
3.	table	(command)	________________

PRACTICE SENTENCES

Practice Sentences–1

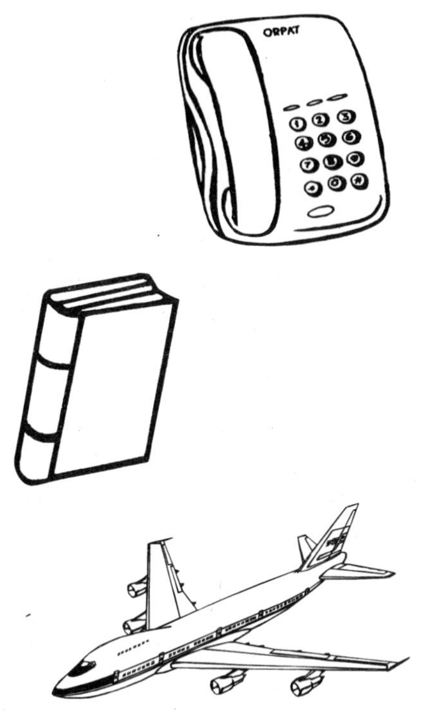

This is a telephone.

That is a telephone bell.

That's a telephone bell.

That is a pen.

That's a pen.

That is a book.

That's a book.

That is an aeroplane.

What is this?

That is a pen.

What is this?

That is a door.

What is that?

That is a bell.

Practice Sentences–2

This is a room.

That's a wall.

That's a window.

That's a lamp.

This is a pen, and this is a pencil.

That is a box.

These are bills.

This is a dog. These are dogs.

That is an aeroplane. Those are aeroplanes.

These are books.

This is a match. These are matches.

That is a box. Those are boxes.

What are these?

What are those?

Those are dogs.

What are these?

These are pencils.

What are those?

Those are oranges.

These are walls, and those are windows.

This is a telephone bell, and those are aeroplanes.

Practice Sentences–3

This is a window.

Is this a window?

That is a door.

Is that a door?

These are oranges.

Are these oranges?

Is that a bird?

Yes, it is.

Are these bells?

Yes, they are.

Are those lamps?

Yes, they are.

Is this a glass?

No, it is not.

No, it isn't.

Are those glasses?

No, they are not.

No, they aren't.

What is this?a

It's a watch.

What is that?

It's a pencil.

What are these?

These are walls.

What are those?

Those are windows.

Practice Sentences–4

Q. Who is Mr Brown?

A. He is a man.

Q. Who is Mrs Brown?

A. She is a woman.

Q. Who are Dr John and Mr Brown?

A. They are men.

Q. Are Ms Brown and Mary women?

A. Yes, they are.

Q. What do Ms Brown and Mary do?

A. Ms Brown is a housewife, and Mary is a student.

Q. Who is this?

A. This is Edward. He is a doctor.

Q. Who is she?

A. She is Ms Edward. She isn't a doctor.

Q. Who is he?

A. That man is a student.

Q. What does this woman do?

A. This woman is a doctor.

Q. What does those men do?

A. Those men are businessmen.

Q. Who are these women?

A. These women are teachers.

Practice Sentences–5

John: Good morning! Are you Miss Brown?

Mary: Yes, my name is Mary Brown, and you are Dr John, aren't you?

John: Yes. Are those your mother and father?

Mary: Yes, they are my parents. Father, this is Dr John.

Mary's Father: Oh! Good morning Dr John.

4

Conversation

Mr Smith: Good morning, Miss Tailor. How are you?

Miss Tailor: I'm fine, thank you. How are you Mr Smith?

Mr Smith: I'm fine, thank you. Miss Tailor, this is Ms Davis.

Ms Davis: How do you do Miss Tailor?

Miss Tailor: How do you do Ms Davis?

Goodbye, Mr Smith. I'll see you later.

Goodbye, Mr Wilson.

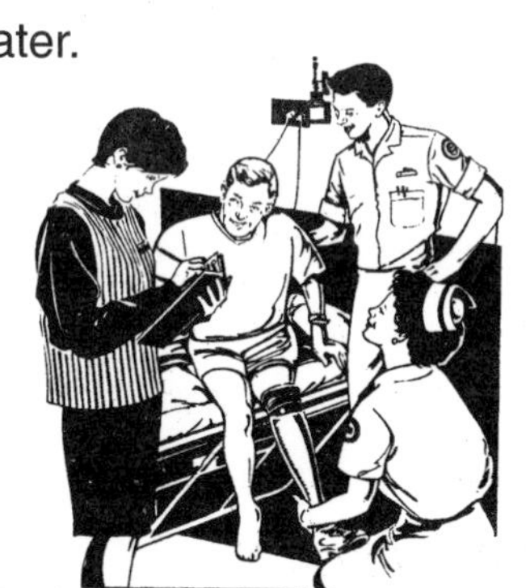

Q. Who are you?

A. I am Miss Davis.
I am a busy nurse.

Q. Who is she?

A. She is Jane.
She is a pretty clerk.

Q. Who is he?

A. He is Dr Smith.
He is an excellent doctor.

Sam: Who are you?

Jack: I am Jack. I am a good student.

Sam: Who are they?

Jack: They are Peter and Mary. They are intelligent students.

A: Who is she?

B: She is an English teacher.

A: Where is she?

B: She is in the classroom.

A: Where are you?

B: We are in the hospital.
We are patients.

A: Who is she?

B: She is an attentive nurse.

A: Where is she?

B: She is at the hospital.

Q. Where are the chairs?

A. They are on the floor.
They are new chairs.

Q. Where is the map?

A. It is on the wall. It's a big map.

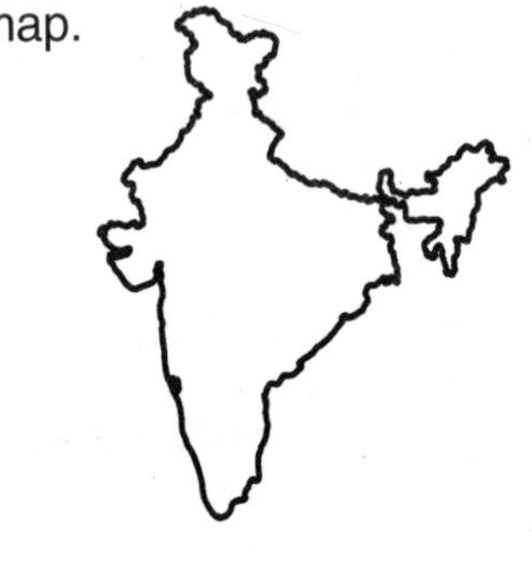

Q. What do you do?

A. I'm a housewife.

Q. Who are they?

A. They are lawyers.

Q. Who is he?

A. He is a dentist.

Q. Do you know what I do?

A. You are a secretary.

Q. Who are we?

A. You are bus drivers.

Mr Drake: Good afternoon, Ms Wilson!

Ms Wilson: Good afternoon, Mr Drake!

Mr Drake: Is Mr Wilson at home?

Ms Wilson: Yes, he is at home. Please come in.

This is the Drakes family.

Mr Drake, Mrs Drake, Bobby Drake and Betsy Drake.

They are our relatives.

This is Mrs Drake. She is Mr Drake's wife.

That is Betsy Drake. She is Mrs Drake's daughter.

This boy is Bobby Drake. He is Betsy's brother.

That is a dog. It is the Drakes' pet dog.

Q. What is your name?

A. My name is John Smith.

Q. How old are you?

A. I'm seventeen years old.

Q. What colour are Mary's eyes?

A. Mary's eyes are blue in colour.

Q. What colour is her hair?

A. She has blonde hair.

Q. Is she tall?

A. No, she is short.

Q. Where are you from?

A. I am from Mexico.

Q. Who is she?

A. She is an English teacher.

Q. Where is she from?

A. She is from Chicago.

Ms Tailor is teaching English.

She is standing.

The students are listening.

They are learning English.

They are writing in the notebook.

They are looking at the teacher.

This is an English class.

Mr Smith is the teacher.

The students are learning English.

Peter is asking a question.

The teacher is answering.

Q. What is he teaching?

A. He is teaching English.

Q. Where are the teacher's books?

A. They are on his desk.

Q. Who are the people in the picture?

A. They are Mr Smith's students.

Q. Who is the student near the map?

A. That is Harry Brown.

Q. What is he doing?

A. He is learning English.

5

Parts of Speech

Words are divided into different kinds or classes called **parts of speech**, according to the work they do in a sentence. There are eight parts of speech:

1. Noun
2. Adjective
3. Pronoun
4. Verb
5. Adverb
6. Preposition
7. Conjunction
8. Interjection

1. A **noun** is the name of a person, place or thing.
2. An **adjective** is a word that describes the noun, telling us about its quality, quantity, size, colour, etc.
3. A **pronoun** is a word used in place of a noun.
4. A **verb** is used to say what a person or thing does, what a person or thing is, or what a person or thing has.
5. An **adverb** is a word that adds to the meaning of a verb, an adjective or another adverb.
6. A **preposition** is a word which shows the relation between a noun or a pronoun and some other words in a sentence.

7. A **conjunction** is used to join words or groups of words or sentences.
8. An **interjection** is a word which expresses some sudden feeling.

Words are divided into different classes according to the work they do in sentences.

E.g. 1. It will **rain** tomorrow. (Verb)
Rain is good for the plants. (Noun)

In the first sentence, 'rain' has been used as an action word, so it has been used as a *verb*.

In the second sentence, 'rain' has been used as the name of something, so it has been used as a *noun*.

E.g. 2. Please don't **box** him hard. (Verb)
This **box** is very heavy. (Noun)

In the first sentence, 'box' has been used as an action word, so it has been used as a *verb*.

In the second sentence, 'box' has been used as the name of something, so it has been used as a *noun*.

EXERCISE 14

Use the following words as verbs and nouns, and make two sentences with each word:

1. work (Noun) ____________________
   work (Verb) ____________________
2. rain (Noun) ____________________
   rain (Verb) ____________________
3. hand (Noun) ____________________
   hand (Verb) ____________________

4. nail (Noun) ____________________________
   nail (Verb) ____________________________
5. box (Noun) ____________________________
   box (Verb) ____________________________
6. watch (Noun) ____________________________
   watch (Verb) ____________________________
7. smoke (Noun) ____________________________
   smoke (Verb) ____________________________
8. apple (Noun) ____________________________
   apple (Verb) ____________________________
9. fan (Noun) ____________________________
   fan (Verb) ____________________________
10. light (Noun) ____________________________
    light (Verb) ____________________________
11. answer (Noun) ____________________________
    answer (Verb) ____________________________
12. drink (Noun) ____________________________
    drink (Verb) ____________________________
13. action (Noun) ____________________________
    action (Verb) ____________________________
14. milk (Noun) ____________________________
    milk (Verb) ____________________________
15. colour (Noun) ____________________________
    colour (Verb) ____________________________

6

Nouns

Types of Nouns

1. **Proper Noun**
2. **Common Noun**
3. **Collective Noun**
4. **Abstract Noun**

1. Name of a particular person or place is called a **proper noun**.
   E.g. New York, London, James, Mary, Japan, Juhi, Sony, Videocon.
2. Common name of a place, person, animal or thing is called a **common noun.**
   E.g. forest, market, boy, girl, elephant, lion, table, chair.
3. When a number of things are taken together and spoken of as one whole, it is called a **collective noun**.
   E.g. Team, crowd, bunch, bouquet.
4. A quality, feeling or idea which we can feel but we cannot touch is called an **abstract noun.**
   E.g. honesty, pain, pleasure, anger.

Kinds of Gender

(*a*) A noun that denotes a male is the **masculine gender.**
E.g. boy, brother, father, prince.

(*b*) A noun that denotes a female is the **feminine gender.**
E.g. girl, sister, mother, princess.

(*c*) A noun that denotes both male and female is the **common gender.**
E.g. cousin, friend, student, baby.

(*d*) A noun that denotes a non-living being is **neuter gender.**
E.g. book, room, plant, pen.

Feminine of nouns are formed in different ways:

1. By using entirely different words—
    1. boy – girl
    2. man – woman
    3. father – mother
    4. brother – sister
    5. son – daughter
2. By adding **ess**—

    1. priest – priestess
    2. lion – lioness
    3. poet – poetess
    4. host – hostess
    5. steward – stewardess

3. Adding **ess** after dropping the vowel of the masculine—

    1. actor – actress
    2. emperor – empress
    3. prince – princess
    4. waiter – waitress
    5. tiger – tigress

4. By placing a word before or after it—
    1. cock sparrow – hen sparrow
    2. he goat – she goat

3. manservant – maidservant
4. grandfather – grandmother
5. landlord – landlady

Singular and Plural

1. Plurals of nouns are generally formed by adding **s** to the singular noun—
    1. boy – boys
    2. book – books
    3. table – tables
    4. chair – chairs
    5. ball – balls
2. Nouns ending in, **'s', 'sh', 'ch'** or **'x'** form the plural by adding **-es** to the singular—
    1. class – classes
    2. dish – dishes
    3. match – matches
    4. tax – taxes
    5. watch – watches
3. Nouns ending in **'o'** form their plural by adding **-es** to the singular—
    1. buffalo – buffaloes
    2. cargo – cargoes
    3. volcano – volcanoes
    4. hero – heroes
    5. mango – mangoes
4. Nouns ending in **'y'** preceded by a consonant form their plural by changing **y** into **ies**.
    1. baby – babies
    2. army – armies
    3. lady – ladies

4. story – stories
5. city – cities

5. Nouns ending in **'f'** form their plural by changing **f** into **v** and adding **es**—
    1. thief – thieves
    2. leaf – leaves
    3. shelf – shelves
    4. calf – calves
    5. wolf – wolves

6. Some plurals are formed by changing the inside vowel of the singular—
    1. man – men
    2. woman – women
    3. tooth – teeth
    4. foot – feet
    5. goose – geese

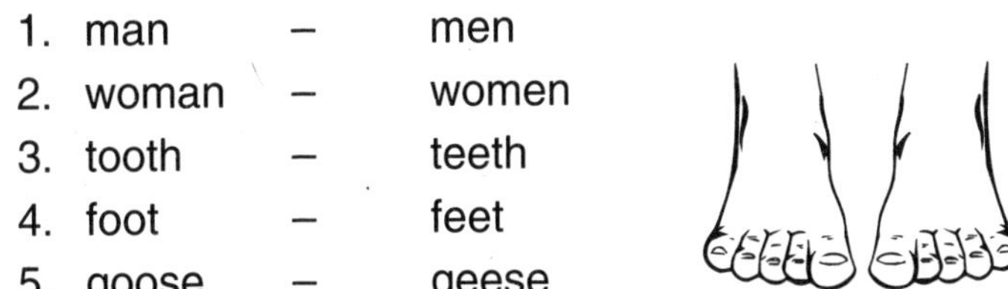

7. Some nouns have their plural and singular alike—
    1. sheep – sheep
    2. deer – deer
    3. dozen – dozen
    4. swine – swine
    5. score – score

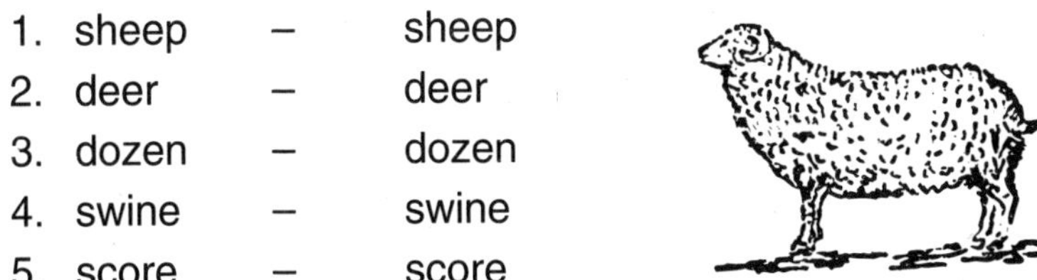

8. Some nouns are used only as plurals—
    1. scissors
    2. trousers
    3. spectacles
    4. billiards
    5. measles

9. Some plural forms are used only in singular—
    1. mathematics
    2. physics

3. politics
4. innings
5. mechanics

10. Some collective nouns, though singular in form, are used as plural—
    1. poultry
    2. dairy
    3. cattle
    4. people
    5. herd

11. Some plurals are formed by adding **s** to the principal word—

1.	daughter-in-law	–	daughters-in-law
2.	commander-in-chief	–	commanders-in-chief
3.	stepson	–	stepsons
4.	maidservant	–	maidservants
5.	son-in-law	–	sons-in-law

EXERCISE 15

Fill in the blanks.

1. We say one wolf but a pack of __________.

2. We say one child but a number of __________.

3. We say one lion but a pride of __________.

4. We say one ship but a fleet of __________.

5. We say one key but a bunch of __________.

6. We say one house but many __________.

7. We say one tooth but a set of __________.

8. We say one shoe but a pair of __________.

9. We say one glove but a pair of __________.

10. We say one flower but a bouquet of __________.

EXERCISE 16

Choose the right word from the brackets.

1. A pack of (lion, lions) attacked the cow.
2. Put these (pen, pens) on the (table, tables).
3. The (goose, geese) have webbed (foot, feet).
4. How many (medal, medals) have you won?
5. He had to pay for many (horse, horses) for that (holiday, holidays).
6. We have two big (toe, toes) on each (foot, feet).
7. This (colony, colonies) is full of (mosquito, mosquitoes).
8. I need a pair of (scissor, scissors) to cut the (cloth, clothes).
9. Many people wear (spectacles, spectacle).
10. A number of (child, children) are playing in the (school, schools).

EXERCISE 17

Fill in the blanks.

	Singular	**Plural**
1.	church	____________
2.	baby	____________
3.	____________	mice
4.	____________	sheep
5.	____________	storeys
6.	ox	____________
7.	fox	____________
8.	____________	teeth
9.	____________	wives

10. office ____________
11. fairy ____________
12. ____________ geese
13. hero ____________
14. ____________ feet
15. deer ____________
16. roof ____________
17. ____________ families
18. wolf ____________
19. child ____________
20. shelf ____________

EXERCISE 18

Change the underlined words into their plural form.

1. The tiger killed the deer. ________ ________
2. The child followed the woman. ________ ________
3. Put the pencil on the shelf. ________ ________
4. The policeman caught the thief. ________ ________
5. Please tell the child sitting on the bench. ________ ________
6. The lady played the piano. ________ ________
7. The leader of the army fought a war. ________ ________
8. The magician carries a handkerchief. ________ ________
9. We can learn from the life of a great man. ________ ________
10. The servant swept the floor. ________ ________

EXERCISE 19

Make the nouns in the following sentences plural:

1. Bring your knife, fork and spoon from the kitchen.
2. The tiger has eaten up the deer.
3. Will the hunter shoot that sheep?
4. A rabbit is standing near the burrow.
5. A flower fell from the tree.
6. The mother looks after the baby.
7. A duck swims in the pond.
8. You have received good education from your teacher.
9. That girl plays with a doll along with that child.
10. The mouse easily got into the trap.

EXERCISE 20

Make the nouns in the following sentences singular:

1. Babies suck their thumbs.
2. Lions kill deer.
3. Rabbits eat carrots.
4. Bears eat honey.
5. Four eggs are needed for the breakfast.
6. Children play games.
7. They can't see without their spectacles.
8. His hands are as brown as chestnuts.
9. The mountaineers climbed hills and valleys.
10. The monkeys hang from the branches of trees.

EXERCISE 21

Rewrite the following sentences, changing the underlined nouns from masculine to feminine gender:

1. My uncle will help all the nephews.

   ____

2. The prince rode a black horse.

   ____

3. The lion roared in the jungle.

   ____

4. The man came with a big dog.

   ____

5. The cock sat on the bull.

   ____

6. The husband and the son worked hard.

   ____

7. The king was killed by his brother.

   ____

8. The boy ran after the witch.

   ____

9. The gentleman greeted his father.

   ____

10. 'Sir!' he said to the patron.

    ____

EXERCISE 22

Fill in the blanks.

	Masculine	**Feminine**
1.	actor	________
2.	________	girl
3.	brother	________
4.	cock	________
5.	________	bitch
6.	father	________
7.	________	lady
8.	hero	________
9.	________	mare
10.	husband	________
11.	________	queen
12.	lion	________
13.	________	woman
14.	nephew	________
15.	________	princess
16.	sir	________
17.	________	daughter
18.	tiger	________
19.	________	aunt
20.	________	cow
21.	drone	________
22.	________	empress
23.	bachelor	________
24.	________	widow

25. headmaster ____________
26. monk ____________
27. peacock ____________
28. ____________ milkmaid
29. god ____________
30. washerman ____________

EXERCISE 23

Change the gender of the underlined nouns:

1. The <u>bridegroom</u> was very young.

   ____

2. The <u>girl</u> is talking about her <u>uncle</u>.

   ____________ ____________

3. The <u>peacock</u> danced near the <u>horse</u>.

   ____________ ____________

4. My <u>sister-in-law</u> is a <u>poetess</u>.

   ____________ ____________

5. The <u>hostess</u> greeted my <u>grandfather</u>.

   ____________ ____________

6. The <u>author</u> was praised by the <u>queen</u>.

   ____________ ____________

7. The <u>lady</u> and her <u>manservant</u> are buying vegetables.

   ____________ ____________

8. Her <u>landlord</u> was visited by a friend.

   ____

9. The <u>priest</u> prayed to God.

   ____

10. The <u>salesman</u> sold a ring to the <u>princess</u>.

    ___________ ___________

EXERCISE 24

Fill in the blanks with one of the following words:

zoo, sty, kennel, hive, den, barrack, convent, burrow, pen, stable.

1. Soldiers live in a ___________.
2. Lions live in a ___________.
3. Rabbits live in a ___________.
4. Dogs live in a ___________.
5. Nuns live in a ___________.
6. Wild animals are kept in a ___________.
7. Farm animals are kept in a ___________.
8. Bees live in a ___________.
9. Horses live in a ___________.
10. Pigs live in a ___________.

EXERCISE 25

Fill in the blanks with appropriate words:

schools, stage, rails, gardens, chimney, tunnel, branches, hose, kitchen, trees.

1. Trains run on ___________.
2. Children study in ___________.
3. The actors act on the ___________.

4. Flowers grow in ____________.
5. The train passes through a ____________.
6. Smoke passes through a ____________.
7. Monkeys swing on ____________.
8. Mother cooks in the ____________.
9. Water passes through a ____________.
10. Apples grow on ____________.

Countable and Uncountable Nouns

Read the following countable nouns loudly:

Book	Pencil	Pen
Hand	Finger	Television
Chair	Table	Door
Window	Cushion	Quilt
Apple	Banana	Papaya
House	Car	Curtain
Boy	Girl	Bottle
Plate	Flower	Computer
Shirt	Frock	Box
Cows	Deer	Cycle
Cupboard	Tree	Sharpener
Diary	Painting	Carpet
Bed	Lock	Bedsheet
Dictionary	Bag	Key

Read the following uncountable nouns loudly:

Milk	Rain	Air
Water	Electricity	Sky
Oxygen	Gas	Sand
Wheat	Rice	Oil

Sugar	Dust	Grass
Smoke	Steam	Thunder
Cold	Heat	Freedom
Childhood	Knowledge	Happiness
English	Sadness	Blood
Attention	Punishment	Misery
Business	Geography	Lava
History	Colour	Beauty
Imagination	Sorrow	Atmosphere
Glory	Salt	Politeness

EXERCISE 26

State whether the following words are countable nouns or uncountable (Write C for countable and U for uncountable).

1.	Ink	______	**11.**	Brick	______
2.	Book	______	**12.**	Slice	______
3.	Milk	______	**13.**	Rupee	______
4.	Pain	______	**14.**	Money	______
5.	Rain	______	**15.**	Coin	______
6.	Sheet	______	**16.**	Chalk	______
7.	Cloth	______	**17.**	Honesty	______
8.	Water	______	**18.**	Anger	______
9.	Paper	______	**19.**	Air	______
10.	Register	______	**20.**	Finger	______

7

Conversation

Q. Is the lesson interesting?
A. Yes, it is.
Q. Are you listening to the teacher?
A. Yes, I am.

Q. What time is it?
A. It is 2 O'clock.
Q. Is your watch right?
A. No, it is five minutes slow.

Q. What time is it?
A. It's 3 O'clock.
Q. What time is it?
A. It's nine thirty.
Q. What time is it?
A. It is quarter to three.
Q. What time is it?
A. It is five fifteen.
Q. What time is it?
A. It's one O'clock.

Q. What time is it?

A. It's time to leave.
It's time to begin.
It's time to eat.
It's time to go.

Ms Wilson gets up at six thirty.
She dresses.
She fixes breakfast.
Mr Wilson gets up at seven O'clock.
He takes a shower and shaves.
He leaves for work at eight thirty.
The children get up at seven thirty.
They comb their hair.
They brush their teeth.
They leave for school at eight forty.
School begins at 9 O'clock.

Q. What time do the children get up?

A. The children get up at seven thirty.

Q. What time does Mr Wilson have breakfast?

A. He has breakfast at around eight O'clock.

Q. What time does Ms Wilson fix breakfast?

A. She fixes breakfast at seven thirty.

Q. What time is it?

A. It is seven O'clock.

Q. What is Ms Wilson doing?

A. She is fixing breakfast for her family.

Q. What time does her husband leave for work?

A. He leaves for work at eight thirty.

A: May I help you?

B: Yes, I'd like to see some coats.

A: What size do you wear?

B: I wear size fourteen.

A: Is there any specific colour that you are looking for?

B: No, any nice colour would do.

A: OK. Please come this way.

Mr Wilson is an American.

He lives in a small town in the United States.

He works in a clothing store.

He sells men's clothes.

He makes a good salary.

He has many customers.

He goes to work at 9 O'clock every morning.

The store opens at 10 O'clock.

George: Good morning Mr Wilson.

Wilson: Good morning Mr George.

George: I need a new hat.

Wilson: What size do you wear?

George: I wear size seven.

Wilson: We have this hat in size seven. Try it on.

George: It fits fine. How much does it cost?

Wilson: It is twenty-five dollars and seventy-five cents.

George: Do you accept credit card?

Wilson: Yes, we do accept it.

George: Here is my credit card.

Wilson: Please sign here.
Here is your package.
Your receipt is inside.
Come again.
Goodbye.

George: Thank you.

Where does Mr Wilson live?

He lives in a small town.

He is wearing a red tie today.

What size is his shirt?

It's size sixteen.

That is Mrs Wilson.

She is wearing a pretty skirt.

I like her purse.

Mr John's suit is grey.

I don't like Sarah's blouse.

Jack is wearing a black leather belt.

8

Pronouns

A **pronoun** is a word used instead of a noun.

Pronoun can be singular or plural.

Pronoun can be masculine or feminine.

It can be common or neuter gender just like nouns.

1. Personal pronoun

(*a*) The first person is the person who is speaking, *i.e.* I, me, we, us.

I and **me** are singular. **We** and **us** are plural. They can be used for both males and females and are common gender.

(*b*) The second person is the person spoken to, *i.e.* you and yours. **You** and **yours** can be used as singular and plural and are common gender since they can be used for both males and females.

The third person is the person spoken about, *i.e.* he, him, she, her, it, they, them.

He and **him** are singular and are used for males. **She** and **her** are singular and are used for females. **It** is singular and is used for animals and non-living things. **They** and **them** are plural and are used for males, females, animals and non-living things.

2. A pronoun that is used to point out the object or objects to which it refers is called a **demonstrative pronoun.**

   E.g. **This** is a pencil.
   These are pencils.

3. A pronoun that is used to ask a question is called an **interrogative pronoun**.

   E.g. **What** do you want?
   Which is your coat?

4. The pronouns myself, ourselves, yourself, yourselves, himself, herself, itself and themselves when used as the receiver of an action are called **reflexive pronouns**.

   E.g. I enjoyed **myself**.
   He helped **himself**.

5. A pronoun used to convey emphasis is called an **emphatic pronoun**.

   E.g. I **myself** saw her crying.
   She **herself** told me about it.

6. A pronoun that shows possession is called a **possessive pronoun.**

   E.g. This house is **yours**.
   That car is **mine**.

EXERCISE 27

Encircle the personal pronouns in the following sentences:

1. They do not care about him.
2. Will he tell us his views?
3. He said to me, "Is this your house or mine?"
4. You thanked us for all that we had done for you.
5. You need not worry. I can do it just now.
6. Her mother gave them one chocolate each.
7. She loves them very much.

8. He asked him to come back at 8 O'clock.
9. You and your parents are most welcome to stay with us.
10. I like this book, so please give it to me.

EXERCISE 28

Use pronouns in place of the underlined words.

1. Joe and John are brothers. Joe and John are going to see a movie. Joe and John will come back at 11 p.m.
2. When the dog saw an old man, the dog started barking at the old man. The old man ran away from the dog. The old man did not come back again.
3. Neha is a singer. Neha sings very well. Last night Neha sang at a party. Everybody praised Neha.
4. Mary has many books. Mary likes to read new books. Mary does not lend her books to anyone. Mary has a big library in her house.
5. Amy went to James's party. Amy presented an interesting book to James. James thanked Amy. James and Amy are good friends.

EXERCISE 29

Fill in the blanks with appropriate reflexive pronouns.

1. He hurt __________ in an accident.
2. I checked __________ at once.
3. The elephant hurt __________.
4. They enjoyed __________ in the market.
5. The cat covered __________ with dirt.
6. I saw __________ in the mirror.
7. They cleaned the room __________.

8. She picked up all the books __________.
9. He prepared the food __________.
10. We must do all the work __________.

EXERCISE 30

Rewrite the following sentences, using possessive pronouns:

E.g. This book belongs to me.
This book is mine.

1. These clothes belong to her.
____
2. This is her box.
____
3. That is your camel.
____
4. These houses belong to you.
____
5. This car belongs to him.
____
6. That is my shop.
____
7. They own this farm.
____
8. He owns this ranch.
____

9. She owns this hotel.

____

10. This computer belongs to him.

____

EXERCISE 31

Read the following sentences, and tick the correct pronoun:

1. He will invite (she, her) to his house.
2. They enjoyed (them, themselves) at the wedding reception.
3. She has met (him, he) many a times.
4. You work as hard as (I, me) do.
5. He is taller than (I, me).
6. It is your duty not (my, mine) to look after the baby.
7. He (him, himself) told me that he is married.
8. I will go to my hotel. You go to (your, yours).
9. David and (me, I) went to meet (him, himself).
10. He has invited (her, herself) many a times.

EXERCISE 32

Fill in the following blanks with correct pronouns:

1. If the children are ready, take __________ for a movie.
2. The girl was ill, so I took __________ to the doctor.
3. You can't blame __________, as I was not responsible for it.
4. They __________ asked me to come.
5. Here are your toys. __________ are all useless. Take __________ away.

6. "This bicycle is ____________," announced the two children.
7. The teacher said, "_________ have asked _________ many a times to tell the truth."
8. Jenny has a big doll. The whole day __________ likes to play with __________.
9. Are these my books or __________?
10. When all the guests come, give the presents to __________.

EXERCISE 33

Fill in the blanks with *what, whom, who, where.*

1. __________ do you want?
2. __________ does she like?
3. __________ are they?
4. __________ do they stay?
5. __________ won the match?
6. __________ is the dacoit?
7. __________ did the old lady see?
8. __________ broke the glass?
9. __________ shall we tell him?
10. __________ would you like to do?
11. __________ are those ladies?
12. __________ did the princes love?
13. __________ is your name?
14. __________ is your car?
15. __________ do you like?

9

Conversation

Q. Where do you live?

A. I live in Springfield.

Q. What's your address?

A. My address is 316 Nash street.

The Wilsons arrived in Springfield between three and four O'clock.

They looked for State street.

Ms Wilson's parents lived at 625 East State Street. But now her parents live at 369 Park Avenue.

They easily found Park Avenue.

The Johnson's house was at the corner of the Park Avenue.

Mr Wilson parked the car in front of the house.

Ms Johnson came out of the house and greeted them.

Ms Wilson: Hello Mum!

Ms Johnson: Hello everybody, get out of the car and come in. We were expecting you at two thirty, it is almost four O'clock now.

Ms Wilson: Well, Texi and Bobby were hungry, so we stopped to eat lunch. That delayed us a little. But, the trip wasn't long. We started at eight thirty this morning.

Take the suitcase and boxes out of the car. Carry this suitcase, Bobby. Take this box, Texi. I will carry the rest.

Ms Johnson: Did you enjoy your trip?

Ms Wilson: Yes, we enjoyed it very much.
The scenery was beautiful.
The trees and grass were very green.

Ms Johnson: There are lots of flowers at this time of the year.

Ms Wilson: So, this is your new house? It is very attractive.

Ms Johnson: Yes, we moved here last month.
I'm going to show you around. Put your things down, and come with me.

Ms Wilson: You have arranged your furniture nicely, and I like the colour of your wallpaper and the rugs. You certainly have a charming house.

Ms Johnson is pleased with her new home.

It's a two-storey house with ten rooms.

There are three bedrooms on the ground floor.

There are four rooms on the first floor.

There are three rooms on the second floor. She happily shows her visitors around.

Ms Wilson: Didn't you buy new furniture for your house?

Ms Johnson: We bought some new furniture for the living room, but we didn't buy any furniture for the other rooms. We are using the furniture from the old house.

Ms Wilson: The bookcases look new.

Ms Johnson: Your father painted them. They are green now. Earlier they were brown.

Ms Wilson: I recognise the couch and the chairs. When did you get the television?

Ms Johnson: Oh yes! The television is new. We got it last month. We also have three bedrooms upstairs.

Ms Wilson: That's good.

Ms Johnson: There are many closets too. The house is very large. We have a lot of room for guests now.

The Johnson's house is very large.

It has two floors.

There are three bedrooms on the ground floor, four bedrooms on the first floor and three bedrooms on the second floor.

The kitchen is next to the dining room.

There is a refrigerator, a sink and a stove in the kitchen.

Ms Johnson's bedroom is on the ground floor.

There is a bed in her bedroom.

There is a sofa in the living room.

The sofa is between the chair and the piano.

There is a beautiful rug on the floor.

There is a large chair next to the fireplace.

Q. What's in the dining room?

A. There is a table in the dining room.
There are six chairs around the table.
There are some flowers on the table.

Q. What's in the bathroom?

A. There is a bathtub in the bathroom.
There is a toilet next to the sink.
There are few towels on a rack.
There is a mirror over the sink.

Q. Is there a sink under the mirror?

A. Yes, there is.

Q. Are there three chairs in the living room?

A. No, there aren't.

Q. Is there a coffee table in front of the sofa?

A. No, there isn't.

Q. Are there two lamps in the bedroom?

A. No, there is only one.

Q. Are there three pictures on the walls in the living room?

A. No, there aren't. There is only one.

Q. Is this apartment on the second floor for rent?

A. Yes, it is.

Q. How many bedrooms does it have?

A. It has three bedrooms.

Q. What is the rent?

A. It is three hundred and fifty dollars a month.

10

Adjectives

Adjectives are words which describe the noun. They tell us the quality, quantity, kind, size, etc. of the persons, places, animals and things. Adjectives are usually placed before the nouns, but sometimes they may be placed after the nouns.

1. An adjective which tells us of what kind a noun is, is called an **adjective of quality**.

   E.g. The **young** man crossed the **deep** river.

2. An adjective which tells us how much of a thing is meant is called an **adjective of quantity**.

   E.g. John has **enough** money with him.

3. An adjective which tells us how many persons or things are meant is called an **adjective of number**.

   E.g. I have **four** pencils.

4. An adjective which is used to point out some person or thing is called a **demonstrative adjective**.

   E.g. **This** book is interesting.

5. An adjective which used to ask a question is called an **interrogative adjective**.

   E.g. **Whose** house is that?

6. An adjective that shows possession or belonging is called a **possessive adjective**.

   E.g. This is **my** bag.

EXERCISE 34

Underline the adjectives in the following sentences:

MARCH					
Monday	31	3	10	17	24
Tuesday		4	11	18	25
Wednesday		5	12	19	26
Thursday		6	13	20	27
Friday		7	14	21	28
Saturday	1	8	15	22	29
Sunday	**2**	**9**	**16**	**23**	**30**

1. Alexander was a kind ruler.
2. The path was narrow.
3. March has thirty-one days.
4. Always drink pure water.
5. A mosquito is a tiny insect.
6. Leena has black hair.
7. Tiger is a wild animal.
8. New York is a big city.
9. It is a sunny day.
10. The house is beautiful.
11. The pistol went with a loud noise.
12. London is a busy city.
13. The rich man has one child.
14. Gorilla is a dangerous animal.
15. Lincoln was a popular leader.

EXERCISE 35

Write three adjectives to describe the following nouns:

e.g. city — **large, crowded, noisy**.

1. box ____________ ____________ ____________
2. flower ____________ ____________ ____________
3. servant ____________ ____________ ____________
4. house ____________ ____________ ____________
5. book ____________ ____________ ____________

EXERCISE 36

Add a noun to each of the following adjectives:

1. A hard ____________
2. The square ____________
3. A broken ____________
4. A healthy ____________
5. A naughty ____________
6. A shy ____________
7. An interesting ____________
8. A tiny ____________
9. A huge ____________
10. A hot ____________

EXERCISE 37

Underline the adjectives, and write their opposites in the blanks. Choose from the words given below:

loose, dishonest, foolish, narrow, light, blunt, poor, active, stale, quiet, short, easy.

1. The road is wide. ____________
2. He wears tight clothes. ____________
3. She only buys fresh vegetables. ____________
4. They have honest servants. ____________
5. He cuts vegetables with a sharp knife. ____________
6. The monkey has a long tail. ____________
7. The student could not answer the difficult question. ____________
8. She is a lazy woman. ____________
9. The boy was carrying a heavy bag. ____________

10. The hall was very noisy. __________

11. He is a rich man. __________

12. He was a wise man. __________

Adjectives: Degrees of Comparison

Adjectives have three degrees of comparison:

1. Positive
2. Comparative
3. Superlative

1. **Positive degree** is used when we are not making any comparison.
   E.g. great, bright, high.
2. **Comparative degree** is used when we are comparing two persons or things.
   E.g. greater, brighter, higher.
3. **Superlative degree** is used when we are comparing more than two things.
   E.g. greatest, brightest, highest.

Changing Positive Degree to Comparative and Superlative Degree

1. Most adjectives form their comparative degree by adding **-er** and their superlative degree of by adding **-est** to the positive.

Positive (for one)	**Comparative (for two)**	**Superlative (for more than two)**
rich	richer	richest
brave	braver	bravest
tall	taller	tallest
small	smaller	smallest
poor	poorer	poorest

2. If the positive ends in **'e',** we add **r** to the comparative and **st** to the superlative form.

strange	stranger	strangest
brave	braver	bravest
wise	wiser	wisest
fine	finer	finest
pure	purer	purest

3. If the positive ends in **'y'** and has a consonant immediately before it, the **y** is changed into **i** before adding **er** to the comparative and **est** to the superlative. But if **y** has a vowel before, it is not changed into **i** for making the comparative and superlative degrees.

happy	happier	happiest
easy	easier	easiest
heavy	heavier	heaviest
grey	greyer	greyest
gay	gayer	gayest

4. Sometimes the last letter is doubled before adding **er** to the comparative and **est** to the superlative form.

big	bigger	biggest
sad	sadder	saddest
mad	madder	maddest
hot	hotter	hottest
thin	thinner	thinnest

5. Some comparative degrees and superlative degrees are formed by adding **more** to the comparative and **most** to the superlative.

wonderful	more wonderful	most wonderful
beautiful	more beautiful	most beautiful
humble	more humble	most humble

confident	more confident	most confident
important	more important	most important

6. Some degrees of comparisons do not follow any rules; so we learn the comparative and superlative degrees.

bad	worse	worst
good	better	best
little	less	least
many	more	most
far	farther	farthest

***Note*: Use of little, few** and **much, many**

Little is an adjective of quality; **few** is an adjective of number:

E.g. a little water, a little milk,
a few books, a few students.

Much is an adjective of quantity, whereas **many** is an adjective of number.

E.g. much oil, much food
many friends, many books

EXERCISE 38

Fill in the blanks with the correct words.

1. I have ____________ games at home. (much, many)
2. Can you spend ____________ money for me. (a little, a few)
3. The boy has shown ____________ progress in his studies. (much, many)
4. Mary has ____________ relatives than Jone. (fewer, less)
5. We needed ____________ more people to do this work. (a few, a little)

EXERCISE 39

Fill in the blanks with the correct degree of the adjectives given in the brackets:

1. My box is ____________ than yours. (heavy)
2. He has many ____________ friends. (sincere)
3. The tailor was as ____________ as his donkey. (foolish)
4. This is the ____________ lane of this colony. (narrow)
5. Harry's writing is much ____________ than his sister's. (neat)
6. Reha has ____________ friends than her sister. (many)
7. Yesterday was the ____________ day of this season. (hot)
8. This article is the ____________. (bad)
9. This article is ____________ than the one we read yesterday. (bad)
10. This article is ____________. (bad)

EXERCISE 40

Fill in the blanks with possessive adjectives:

1. John is reading ___________ book.
2. The girl is brushing ___________ teeth.
3. The monkey is biting ___________ tail.
4. The cow is feeding ___________ young ones.
5. Joe is talking to ___________ parents.
6. You are talking to ___________ friends.
7. We are talking to ___________ maidservants.
8. They are talking to ___________ parents.
9. I am listening to ___________ brother.
10. She is shouting at ___________ sister.

EXERCISE 41

Fill in the blanks with the correct degree of the adjectives given in the brackets:

1. Kolkata is the ___________ city in India. (big)
2. My handwriting is ___________ than yours. (good)
3. I am ___________ than you. (short)
4. I have ___________ money than you. (much)
5. She is the ___________ of the four sisters. (good)
6. A deer runs ___________ than a hare. (fast)
7. This is the ___________ hall in the school. (big)
8. He is the ___________ man in India. (old)
9. Your article is ___________ than mine. (interesting)
10. Jane is ___________ than Ann. (pretty)
11. Rita is the ___________ of the three friends. (tall)
12. The principal is ___________ than the teachers. (wise)
13. Gold is ___________ than copper. (useful)
14. Florida is ___________ from New York than Washington. (far)
15. Mount Everest is the ___________ peak. (high)
16. This writing is ___________ than your last one. (bad)
17. Reena is a ___________ person than her mother. (good)
18. He is the ___________ popular boy in his class. (more)
19. The Browns are ___________ than the Davids. (nice)
20. He is ___________ than his cousin. (fat)

EXERCISE 42

Complete the following sentences with the correct degree of the adjectives given in the brackets:

1. Jane is the __________ of the two girls. (short)
2. This animal is ugly but that one is __________. (ugly)
3. This hill station is the __________ in the world. (fine)
4. John is the __________ boy in his class. (thin)
5. He knew the __________ about his school. (less)
6. His father was __________ of him than his sister. (proud)
7. She was the __________ girl in her class. (happy)
8. You are __________ than him. (old)
9. This was my __________ day. (worse)
10. It is very __________ today. (coldest)

11

Conversation

A: Good morning!
I'd like to cash this cheque.

B: Do you have an account at the bank?

A: Yes, I do.

B: May I have your account number please?

A: Yes, you can. It is 2934.

B: Thank you. Here is your money.

During their visit to Springfield, the Wilsons' children found many differences between their town and Springfield. Springfield is larger than Greenhill. There are many more interesting things to do in Springfield than in Greenhill. The streets in Springfield are wider than they are in Greenhill. People in Greenhill are friendlier than people in Springfield. There aren't as many stores in Greenhill as there are in Springfield. Shopping is better in Springfield than it is at Greenhill. Clothes and food are not as cheap in Greenhill as they are in Springfield. People in Greenhill do not appear to be as busy as people in Springfield. Springfield has a better transportation system than Greenhill. The traffic is worse in Springfield than it is in Greenhill.

Q. Are there more restaurants and museums in Springfield than there are in Greenhill?

A. Yes, there are.

Q. Is gasoline much expensive in Springfield than it is in Greenhill?

A. Yes, it is.

Q. Are children safer in Springfield than they are in Greenhill?

A. No, they are not.

A. Is there less noise in Greenhill than in Springfield.

A. Yes, there is.

Q. Is Springfield more polluted than Greenhill?

A. Yes, it is.

Q. Are there less taxies and buses in Springfield than in Greenhill.

A. No, they are not.

A. Is there less crime in Greenhill than in Springfield?

A. Yes, there is.

A dialogue with grandfather.

Bobby: Grandfather, how many people live in Springfield?

Grandfather: Oh, there are less than half a million.

Bobby: Springfield is certainly much bigger than Greenhill.
Are there music theatres in Springfield?

Grandfather: Yes, there are.

Bobby: Is there a sports stadium here?

Grandfather: Yes, maybe we can go to a baseball game this weekend.

Bobby: The zoo is bigger than the one we have at home. Can we visit it?

Grandfather: Of course. You have time to go to all these places.

A: Excuse me! How do I get to the pharmacy?

B: Walk three blocks to the traffic light and turn left. The pharmacy is next to the barber's shop.

A: I will find it. Thank you.

Mr Wilson gets sick.

(One morning the family was having breakfast. Mr Wilson wasn't there. He came to the breakfast table late.)

Mr Wilson: I'm sorry, I'm late.
I don't feel well this morning.

Mr Johnson: What's the matter? Didn't you sleep well?

Mr Wilson: No, I didn't sleep well. I have fever, headache and a terribly sore throat.

Mr Johnson: A cold is going to ruin your vacation with us. I'm going to make an appointment with Dr. Adams. I'm sure he can see you today.

Telephonic Conversation

Mr Johnson: Hello! Is this Dr. Adam's office?

Joan: Yes, it is. This is Miss Joan speaking. What can I do for you?

Mr Johnson: This is Ms Johnson. I would like to make an appointment with Dr. Adam.

Joan: When can you come?

Mr Johnson: Oh no, the appointment isn't for me. It is for Mr Wilson, my son-in-law. Please tell Dr. Adam it is urgent.

(The nurse spoke to Dr. Adam. Then she returned to the telephone.)

Joan: Hello, Mr Johnson. The doctor can see Mr Wilson this afternoon at two. Is that convenient for him?

Mr Johnson: Yes, that would be fine.

Joan: We will see him then.

Mr Johnson: Thank you, goodbye.

(The Johnsons and the Wilsons are in the dining room. They are having lunch. It is twelve thirty. Ms Johnson reminds Mr Wilson about his appointment with the doctor.)

Ms Johnson: Don't forget your appointment with the doctor at two O'clock!
We are going to cancel our visit to the zoo.

Ms Wilson: Oh no! Don't cancel your visit to the zoo. The children will be disappointed. I will take a bus to Dr. Adam's clinic.

12

Verbs

A verb is used to say what a person or thing does, what a person or thing is or what a person or thing has. Verbs show the present time, the past time and the future time.

e.g. run, jump, sleep, eat, drink.

Is, are, am refer to present time; **was, were** refer to past time; **will, shall** refer to future time.

Have shows possession. **Have** and **has** refer to present time. **Had** refers to the past time. **Will have** and **shall have** refer to the future time.

1. A verb that requires an object to complete its sense is called a **transitive verb.**

   e.g. James likes chocolates.
   Mary wastes food.

2. A verb that does not require an object to make sense is called an **intransitive verb**.

   e.g. Ann worked.
   The children played.

3. A verb that requires another word to complete its sense is called a **verb of incomplete predication.** The word which is required to complete the meaning of the verb of incomplete predication is called **complement to the verb.**

   e.g. John is happy.
   The principal appears pleased.

Verbs: Singular and Plural

A singular noun or pronoun takes a singular verb with it, and a plural noun or pronoun takes a plural verb with it.

A verb must agree with its subject in number and persons.

A verb is the heart of sentence.

e.g.

	Subject		**Verb**
Singular:	My frock		is clean.
Plural:	My frocks		are clean.
Singular:	The child		was intelligent.
Plural:	The children		were intelligent.
Singular:	The boy		has toys.
Plural:	The boys		have toys.
Singular:	This child		cries a lot.
Plural:	These children		cry a lot.
Singular:	I	am	sleeping.
Plural:	We	are	sleeping.
Singular:	I	was	sleeping.
Plural:	We	were	sleeping.
Singular:	I	have	slept.
Plural:	We	have	slept.
Singular:	I	do	work.
Plural:	We	do	work.
Plural:	You	are	sleeping.
Plural:	You	were	sleeping.
Plural:	You	have	slept.
Plural:	You	do	work.
Singular:	He	is	sleeping.
Singular:	She	is	sleeping.

Singular:	It	is	sleeping.
Plural:	They	are	sleeping.
Singular:	He	was	sleeping.
Singular:	She	was	sleeping.
Singular:	It	was	sleeping.
Plural:	They	were	sleeping.
Singular:	He	has	slept.
Singular:	She	has	slept.
Singular:	It	has	slept.
Plural:	They	have	slept.
Singular:	He	does	work.
Singular:	She	does	work.
Singular:	It	does	work.
Plural:	They	do	work.

Rule 1. If two singular nouns or pronouns are joined by 'and', they become plural. So they take a plural verb.

E.g. James and Joe are friends.
He and she have gone for a movie.

Rule 2. A collective noun when used as a single unit takes a singular verb.

E.g. Our team has lost the match.
Our class was praised.

Rule 3. If two or more nouns are joined by 'or' or 'nor', they take a singular verb.

E.g. No boy or girl was willing to stay back.
Neither Sarah nor Joan is coming with us.

Rule 4. Nouns singular in meaning but plural in form take singular verb.

E.g. This news is not true.

EXERCISE 43

Fill in the blanks with *is, are* or *am.*

1. It _______ very hot today.
2. I ________ afraid of the dark.
3. I don't like them because they _______ liars.
4. Our players ________ ready for the match.
5. You _______ always late.
6. All my brothers and sisters ________ here.
7. The owner of these houses _____________ a successful businessman.
8. 'Gone with the Wind' _________ a very interesting novel.
9. Iron and ore _________ used for making many things.
10. The news of his promotion ________ really great.

EXERCISE 44

Rewrite these sentences in the singular form. One has been done for you.

1. We are not careless.
   I am not careless.
2. Those books are mine.

   ____
3. The plates are in the kitchen.

   ____
4. These men are young.

   ____

5. These doors are very strong.

____

6. Those orchards are full of fruits.

____

7. They are good children.

____

8. We are learning English.

____

9. You are nice girls.

____

10. They are busy sailors.

____

EXERCISE 45

Fill in the blanks with *was* or *were.*

1. Last year I __________ the head girl.
2. Class X __________ happy with the new teacher.
3. All the students in the class __________ happy with the principal.
4. The ships __________ ready to sail.
5. Many tigers __________ in danger.
6. Harry and Bob __________ my only friends.
7. All the vegetables __________ for sale.
8. Even the youngest man in the crowd __________ not ready to help.
9. I did not buy those mushrooms because they _______ stale.
10. The whole farm __________ his.

EXERCISE 46

Fill in the blanks with *has* or *have.*

1. She ________ never obeyed her mother.
2. Many people __________ gathered outside her house.
3. I __________ a brilliant idea.
4. She __________ her breakfast very early.
5. We __________ a new car.
6. These days some people __________ two cars.
7. Each student in my class __________ a dictionary.
8. Tom and Sam __________ balloons in their hands?
9. The child __________ a toy in her hand.
10. All the school children __________ flags in their hands.

EXERCISE 47

Tick the correct word:

1. She (spend, spends) six hours in the office every day.
2. Last year, this boy (was, were) very weak.
3. Joe and he (play, plays) matches regularly.
4. My friend (teach, teaches) in this school.
5. There (is, are) no beggars on the road.
6. Her parents (quarrel, quarrels) with each other.
7. The old lady standing near the park (is, are) my mother.
8. One of the dacoits (has, have) a car.
9. Old books (is, are) for sale today.
10. Each of these officers (work, works) hard.

EXERCISE 48

Complete the following sentences with the given verbs:

doze, push, drain, doubt, practise, jump, laugh, caught, swing, knock.

1. The girls liked to __________ on the bed.
2. Most rivers __________ into the sea.
3. It is dangerous to __________ each other from behind.
4. Do not let the dog __________ on the chair.
5. The monkeys will __________ on the branches.
6. Do not __________ at the old man.
7. The policeman did not __________ at the door.
8. The thieves were __________ by the inspector.
9. The girl did not __________ on the cassio.
10. I do not __________ your promise.

EXERCISE 49

Use the correct form of the verb to fill in the following blanks:

1. He was __________ in the car. (sat, sitting)
2. The man was __________ on the road. (stand, standing)
3. The jewels were __________ in the basket. (hide, hidden)
4. The shirt was __________ in the wardrobe. (hang, hanging)
5. I. __________ nothing to help him. (did, done)

EXERCISE 50

Fill in the blanks using *done* or *do* (present), *did* (past) *have/has/had done* (past participle).

1. I __________ the work you had asked me to do.
2. The boy __________ his homework before going to school.
3. Have you __________ it or not?
4. She has never __________ household work before.
5. She __________ not know him.
6. The work has not been __________ by my helper.
7. Joe __________ well in the last examination.
8. When __________ he decide to leave?
9. He __________ well in his profession.
10. What __________ he want from me?

EXERCISE 51

see (Present)	saw (Past)	has/have/had seen (Past participle)

Fill in the blanks with the correct form of the verb 'see'.

1. Will you please __________ to it that the work is done.
2. The girls __________ this movie a few days back.
3. He has not __________ his mother today.
4. Did he also __________ what we __________?
5. We have __________ something which we have never __________ before.
6. The old man has __________ better days.
7. He __________ all the old photographs.

8. I can __________ very well with my left eye.
9. I __________ all the programmes on the television.
10. I __________ him at the station.

Can and May

Can means be able to.

May is used to give or ask for permission.

e.g. Can you play tennis? (able to)
May I do this? (permission)

In the past tense, **can** becomes **could** and **may** becomes **might.**

EXERCISE 52

Fill in the blanks, using *can, could, may* or *might* according to the sense.

1. __________ I be excused from attending the party?
2. Perhaps I __________ go for the show tomorrow.
3. __________ you ride the bicycle now?
4. You __________ go and meet the principal any time.
5. My mother said that I __________ stay out till 10 p.m.
6. I __________ come to your house, but I __________ not stay for dinner.
7. I __________ get up at any time of the night.
8. I __________ help the needy because I have enough money.
9. I __________ have asked him to come regularly.
10. __________ I dance with you?

Shall and Will

We use **SHALL** and **WILL** with verbs to show the future tense.

Shall is used with 'you' and 'I'.

Will is used with 'you', 'they', 'he', 'she', 'it'.

If we want to express strong determination, threat or refusal, we use **WILL** with **I** and **we** and **SHALL** with other persons.

e.g. I will marry him, and you shall not stop me.

EXERCISE 53

Fill in the blanks, using *shall* and *will* correctly:

1. "They __________ pay back every penny," shouted the old man.
2. "I __________ come with you even if you don't want me to," declared the stubborn child.
3. We __________ go for the party even if you don't give permission.
4. "He __________ never come here again," I warned my son.
5. "I __________ always wait for her," insisted the lover.

Should and Would

When we want to say that something may possibly happen or is likely to occur, instead of the normal future tense, we need a **conditional tense**. So, instead of **shall** and **will**, we say **should** and **would**.

Should is used almost the same way as shall, *e.g.*

I should not be happy with your behaviour.

Would is used almost the same way as will, *e.g.*

He would live in the city if he could.

Verbs which represent hope or wish, *i.e.*—be glad, like, prefer, are used with **should** and **would**, *e.g.*

They would prefer to go out alone.

Actions that were habits of the past also take **would**, *e.g.*

We would go for shopping every day.

Should is used to express duty, *e.g.*

Every member of the staff should attend the meeting.

EXERCISE 54

Fill in the blanks with *should* or *would*.

1. How much __________ I pay?
2. __________ I reply to his letter?
3. __________ you please close the window?
4. __________ you like to have some tea?
5. __________ you go in your car?
6. On many days, he __________ come home at midnight.
7. Very often he __________ walk to his office.
8. Sometimes he __________ get very angry with the children.
9. You __________ meet all the parents.
10. I think you __________ buy a new car.

Auxiliaries

Auxiliaries are helping verbs which are used to make many sentences.

These helping verbs are—am, is, are, was, were, does, do, did, have, has, had, can, may, will, shall, should, would, could, might, must, needn't, ought, used to.

EXERCISE 55

Fill in the blanks with the right form of the modal auxiliaries given in the brackets (affirmative or negative).

e.g. I can bowl well, but I *can't* bat equally well. (can)

1. Mary _________ pass, but she _________ get very good marks. (may)
2. The minister _________ come to our village now, but he _________ come when he needs our votes. (will)
3. All the children _________ attend the lecture. They _________ be absent tomorrow. (should)
4. I _________ drive very well on an empty road, but I _________ drive in congested areas. (could)
5. Mr Davis _________ come to meet my mother, but his daughter _________ come. (might)
6. You _________ be polite and respectful, you _________ shout. (must)
7. _________ we meet you every day? No, you _________ meet me every day. (need)
8. How _________ you disobey me? You _________ repeat it. (dare)
9. You _________ to be proud of your children. You _________ tell others about this. (ought)
10. We _________ be proud of our nation. We _________ give ear to rumours. (must)

Verbs: Past and Present

	Present	Past	Past Participle
1.	laugh	laughed	laughed
2.	spend	spent	spent

3. come	came	come
4. write	wrote	written
5. speak	spoke	spoken
6. sell	sold	sold
7. swim	swam	swum
8. take	took	taken
9. wear	wore	worn
10. win	won	won
11. bite	bit	bitten
12. cut	cut	cut

13

Conversation

Robert: Good evening! Ms Jackson.
I am glad to have met you.

Ms Jackson: Thank you. It's nice to have seen you too.
Good night!

Ms Wilson is a housewife.

She usually goes to the supermarket on Fridays.

She is in the kitchen.

She is making a grocery list.

She looks in the refrigerator.

She thinks.

I don't have any eggs.

I don't have any milk.

I still have some butter.

I still have some cheese.

She looks in the kitchen cabinets.

She discovers she needs some sugar.

She still has a lot of flour.

She needs a few bananas.

She still has a little rice.

Q. How many oranges does she have?

A. She has a few oranges.

Q. How much bread does she have?

A. She only has a little bread.

Q. How many bars of soaps does she have?

A. She has only a little soap.

Q. How many onions does she have?

A. She still has a lot of onions.

Q. Does she have any potatoes?

A. No, she doesn't.

Q. Does she have meat?

A. No, she doesn't have much meat.

Q. Does she need any carrots?

A. Yes, she needs a few carrots.

Q. Does she need any rice?

A. Yes, she doesn't have much rice.

Q. Does she need any milk?

A. Yes, she doesn't have much milk.

Ms Wilson: Today is Friday.
I am going to the supermarket.
What do you want me to buy?

Eddie: Buy some cookies.
I like chocolate cookies.
Buy some coffee also. We don't have any coffee.
Buy a lot of milk.
We need bread too.
Buy some fruit.
Buy some good meat.

Q. What do you do on Sunday afternoon?

A. I usually go for a movie.

Q. Can I go with you this Sunday?

A. Of course. Meet me at the mall at three fifteen.

No, Mr Wilson usually gets home at five thirty.

He always rests a little while before dinner.

The Wilson family always eats dinner at six O'clock.

Mr Wilson usually reads the newspaper after dinner.

He never washes the dishes after dinner.

The children always do their homework in the evening.

Ms Wilson sometimes has a club meeting on Wednesday afternoons.

The family often watches T.V. together on Sunday evenings.

Mr Wilson is usually busy every morning.

The children are usually hungry at six O'clock.

Mr Wilson is often tired when he gets home.

Bobby is always asleep by ten O'clock.

Q. Do the Wilsons usually stay home in the evenings?

A. Yes, they do.

Q. Doesn't Mr Wilson always read the newspaper before dinner?

A. No, he doesn't.

Q. Isn't he often tired before dinner?

A. Yes, he is.

Q. Aren't the children usually tired by nine O'clock?

A. Bobby isn't.

Q. Doesn't Ms Wilson sometimes have a club meeting during the week?

A. Yes, she does.

Q. Where does Ms Wilson go on Wednesday night?

A. She sometimes goes to a club meeting.

Q. What does Mr Wilson usually read after dinner?

A. He usually reads the newspaper.

Q. Who never washes the dinner dishes?

A. Mr Wilson never washes the dinner dishes.

Q. What time does Bobby usually go to bed?

A. He usually goes to bed at 10 O'clock.

14

Adverbs

An **adverb** is a word that adds to the meaning of a verb, an adjective or another adverb. *E.g.*

1. The dogs barked **loudly**.
2. The boy ran **fast**.
3. The girl sang **sweetly.**
4. She is a **very** intelligent girl.
5. She runs **very** fast.

In the above sentences, **barked, ran, sang** are verbs. The words **loudly, fast** and **sweetly** add to the meaning of the verbs. **Very** adds to the meaning of the adjective 'intelligent' in sentence 4 and **very** adds to the meaning of the adverb 'fast' in sentence 5. These words are called **adverbs**.

1. Adverb of Manner

E.g.
1. The boy slept **soundly**.
2. The old man walked **slowly**.
3. The girl ran **fast.**

In the above sentences, **soundly, slowly** and **fast** describe how certain actions are done. These are **adverbs of manner**. They describe the manner in which actions are done. These adverbs normally answer the question, how?

Most adverbs of manner end in **ly**—

e.g.
1. angry — angrily
2. sad — sadly
3. quick — quickly
4. brave — bravely
5. sweet — sweetly

Some adverbs of manner do not end in **ly**—

e.g.
1. Mary sang **well**.
2. The thief ran **fast**.
3. The lady worked **hard**.

The adverbs **well, fast** and **hard** do not end in **ly**.

These adverbs are placed after the verbs they describe.

2. Adverb of Place

E.g.
1. Joe sat **there**.
2. He is standing **inside**.
3. The beggar looked **up.**

In the sentences given above, **there, inside** and **up** are **adverbs of place**. They tell us where or at what place certain actions are done. They answer the question, where?

3. Adverb of Time

E.g.
1. The boy is sleeping **now**.
2. I was running **then**.
3. I shall study **today**.

In the sentences given above, **now, then** and **today** are **adverbs of time**. They tell us when or at what time certain actions are done.

We can place an adverb of time in the beginning or at the end of the sentence.

E.g. We studied very hard today.

Today we studied very hard.

Adverbs of time answer the question, when?

4. Adverb of Frequency

E.g. 1. I **sometimes** listen to music.

2. He **never** tells a lie.

3. He **always** works hard.

In the sentences given above, **sometimes, never** and **always** are **adverbs of frequency**. An adverb of frequency tells us how often an action is done. It answers the question, how often? An adverb of frequency is placed before the verb if the verb consists of one word. If there is more than one word in the verb, it is placed after the first word.

E.g. I have **never** met him.

I had **always** liked her.

5. Interrogative Adverb

E.g. 1. **When** will you come home?

2. **Where** did you sleep?

3. **Why** are you sad?

4. **How** did you make this dish?

In the above sentences, **when, where, why** and **how** are **interrogative adverbs** since they are used to ask questions.

EXERCISE 56

Underline the adverbs of manner in the following sentences:

1. The baby slept soundly.
2. Rea worked hard.
3. My sister eats fast.
4. My mother spoke softly.
5. He answered wisely.
6. The car moves slowly.
7. Our players played well.
8. My sister was treated badly.
9. The lady cried loudly.
10. The singer sang sweetly.

EXERCISE 57

Underline the adverbs of place in the following sentences:

1. She is sitting outside.
2. He is playing inside.
3. He is waiting downstairs.
4. He has gone far.
5. The sun is above.
6. The beggar has gone somewhere.
7. I looked everywhere.
8. My car was parked on the floor below.
9. He hid underneath a bench.
10. The principal lives here.

EXERCISE 58

Underline the adverbs of time in the following sentences:

1. I woke up early.
2. He will come home soon.

3. She is going to Agra tomorrow.
4. Do the work now.
5. I play daily.
6. We shall eat afterwards.
7. The tailor was paid monthly.
8. He was eating then.
9. He wakes up late.
10. My friend will win today.

EXERCISE 59

Fill in the blanks with suitable adverbs.

1. The soldiers fought ___________.
2. She will come ___________.
3. He is ___________ late.
4. Barking dogs ___________ bite.
5. She wants to go ___________.
6. My new life began ___________.
7. The moon shone ___________.
8. Good children ___________ tell the truth.
9. ___________ will you go?
10. A bullock cart moves ___________.

EXERCISE 60

Fill in the blanks with adverbs opposite in meaning to the ones given in brackets.

1. She sings ___________. (well)
2. Mary does her work ___________. (carelessly)
3. The soldiers fought ___________. (bravely)

4. Smoke moves __________. (upwards)
5. Move forward, don't move __________. (forward)
6. Have you seen a kite go __________? (up)
7. Do you treat your friends __________? (kindly)
8. You need not work __________. (wisely)
9. You should not come home __________. (early)
10. Some of my relatives live __________. (near)

EXERCISE 61

Make adverbs from the following adjectives, and use them in sentences of your own.

1. greedy ______________________________
2. lazy ______________________________
3. quiet ______________________________
4. sincere ______________________________
5. brave ______________________________
6. sound ______________________________
7. patient ______________________________
8. happy ______________________________
9. sad ______________________________
10. willing ______________________________

EXERCISE 62

With one verb, we can use many adverbs.

E.g. eat — greedily, fast, slowly, quickly, silently.
speak — fast, loudly, clearly, softly, slowly, gently, freely.

work — hard, regularly, happily, hardly, willingly, silently, lazily, unwillingly.

Write as many adverbs as you can for the following verbs:

1. play ______________________________
2. walk ______________________________
3. sing ______________________________
4. sleep ______________________________
5. run ______________________________
6. study ______________________________
7. listen ______________________________
8. wait ______________________________
9. look ______________________________
10. pray ______________________________

15

Conversation

A quick lunch

Mr Wilson goes to a fast food restaurant with a friend because he doesn't have much time for lunch.

May I help you?

Yes, a hamburger and a large coke please.

To eat here or take away?

Here.

Pay the cash here at the end of the line, and you sir, what will it be?

Two hotdogs, a cup of hot coffee and a piece of apple pie.

All together it is two fifty.

Thank you, here is your change.

Mr Wilson and his friend carry their tray to a nearby table.

Enough time for lunch.

Today Mr Wilson and his friend have an hour for lunch. They go to a nice restaurant near the store.

They sit down at a table. The waitress brings the menu. She takes their orders.

What will you have?

I will have some beef stew and a cup of coffee.

I will have a club sandwich and a bowl of soup.

The waitress brings two glasses of water.

She puts knives, spoons and forks on the table. She also brings napkins. Then she brings the coffee.

Do you want cream for your coffee?

Yes, I do. Please bring some sugar too.

Here are your orders.

What would you like for dessert?

I'll have a piece of chocolate cake.

Nothing for me. Thanks.

Mr Wilson and his friend finish their lunch. They pay the cheque. They leave a tip for the waitress, and then they go back to work.

Betsy's birthday

Next Sunday is Betsy's birthday. She is going to have a birthday party. She is going to invite her cousins and friends. Her mother is going to bake her a birthday cake. The party is going to be at three O'clock. All her friends are going to come. We are going to buy a nice gift for her. Betsy is going to be nine years old. We will sing a birthday song for her. She is going to blow up the candles on her birthday cake.

Q. Whose birthday is it going to be next Sunday?

A. It's going to be Betsy's birthday.

Q. Is Betsy going to have a party?

A. Yes, she is.

Q. Are her friends and cousins going to come?

A. Yes, they are.

Q. Is the party going to be next Saturday?

A. No, it isn't.

Q. Are you going to buy her a gift?

A. Yes, I am.

Q. Is she going to be twelve years old?

A. No, she isn't.

Q. Where is the party going to be?

A. It's going to be at Betsy's house.

Q. What time is the party going to be?

A. It's going to be at three O'clock.

Q. What is she going to wear at her party?

A. She is going to wear a party dress.

Q. Who is going to come to the party?

A. Her friends and cousins are going to come to the party.

Mother: Betsy, next Sunday is your birthday. Do you want to have a party?

Betsy: Oh yes, that's going to be fun.

Mother: Who are you going to invite?

Betsy: I'm going to invite my friends and cousins.

Mother: I'm going to bake you a beautiful birthday cake. I'm going to buy ice creams and candies too.

Betsy: Are you going to buy any dress for me?

Mother: Yes, I am. Your father is going to buy you a new bicycle too. This is going to be a very special birthday.

16

Prepositions

A **preposition** is a word which is placed before a noun or pronoun to show its relation to some other word mentioned in the sentence.

E.g. The boat sailed **under** the bridge.

Under is a preposition because it shows the connection between boat and bridge.

The train went **through** the tunnel.

Through is a preposition because it shows the connection between train and tunnel.

A preposition is always followed by a noun or pronoun.

Prepositions often express position, cause or direction. They govern the noun or the pronoun which follows them.

Here is a list of commonly used prepositions:

in, on, into, behind, after, under, near, at, into, out, of, over, above, below, from, to, for, in front of, between, among, about, across, against, along, amidst, around, before, beneath, beside, beyond, by, down, during, inside, like, off, upon, opposite, outside, over, past, round, since, through, throughout, till, towards, underneath, unlike, until, up, with, within, without.

EXERCISE 63

Underline the prepositions in the following sentences:

1. The clock <u>on</u> the wall is very beautiful.
2. The little girl is standing behind her father.
3. The corn slipped and fell into the drain.
4. The joker jumped over the fire.
5. The policeman ran after the thief.
6. The poor beggar sat under the tree.
7. He was sitting by the riverside all alone.
8. My friend is waiting at the restaurant.
9. Look at the magician.
10. She cooked dinner for everybody.
11. He passes by our house daily.
12. Many people gathered in front of the rich man's house.
13. Please return before 8 p.m.
14. My daughter is very fond of music.
15. He will write a letter to his father.
16. All the teachers are in the staffroom.
17. He fell from a moving train.
18. I waited at the station.
19. I cannot cut the vegetables with this knife.
20. He is sitting between his parents.

At, on, in are very often used to denote time.

E.g. He slept **at** night.
I will shop **on** Sunday.
The exhibition was held **in** May.

EXERCISE 64

Fill in the blanks with *at, on* or *in*:

1. The exams begin __________ Monday.
2. I shall go home __________ Christmas.
3. It is very hot __________ June.
4. This air is fresh __________ the morning.
5. This building was constructed __________ 1st January, 1948.
6. The prisoner will be free __________ April.
7. __________ summer we wear light clothes.
8. He met me __________ lunch.
9. The show begins __________ 9 p.m.
10. I was awake __________ that time.

In, into, out of are used in the following way:

The water **in** the bottle is hot.

The boy jumped **into** the pool.

When he saw his father, he came **out of** the house.

EXERCISE 65

Fill in the blanks with *in, into* or *out of*:

1. The bear went ________ the cave.
2. He did not find anyone ________ the house.
3. He came ________ the car to meet her.
4. I cannot get ________ the bus just now.
5. My files are ________ the cupboard.
6. Do you have money ________ the bank?
7. Many people are sitting ________ the train.

8. The beggar was not allowed to go ________ the hotel.

9. The blind man fell ________ the well.

10. The principal rushed ________ his office.

On, over, under, above, below can be used in the following ways:

E.g. The book is lying **on** the table.

He has an umbrella **over** his head.

He is standing **under** the tree.

His head is **above** the water.

He is hurt **below** his knee.

EXERCISE 66

Fill in the blanks with *on, over, under, above* or *below*:

1. There are cushions ________ the bed.
2. He jumped ________ the fence.
3. The ship sailed ________ the bridge.
4. The boy swam ________ the bridge.
5. The dog sat ________ the table and licked my feet.
6. There is a bridge ________ the river.
7. He has a pimple just ________ his eye.
8. He held the book just a little ________ his head.
9. The food was lying ________ the table.
10. The hungry boy stood ________ the mango tree, waiting for a ripe mango to drop.

From, to, for are used in the following ways:

E.g. I called her **from** the office.

We stayed in this hotel **for** seven days.

We went **to** the market today.

EXERCISE 67

Fill in the blanks with *from, to* or *for*:

1. My son goes ________ school in the morning.
2. He returned ________ the theatre at 10 p.m.
3. He worked in office ________ the whole day.
4. We stayed in that big house ________ five years.
5. I waited for my mother _______ 8 a.m. _____ 10 a.m.
6. I waited for her ________ two hours.
7. I have not received a birthday card ________ my father.
8. I go ________ college regularly.
9. I bought the storybook ________ my little sister.
10. I waited at the airport ________ two hours.

Behind, in front of, near, between, among are used in the following ways:

E.g. The family members are standing **in front of** their new car.

This dog is walking **behind** his master.

The ball fell **near** the child.

The child happily sat **between** his parents.

The gardener is standing **among** the plants.

EXERCISE 68

Fill in the blanks with *behind, in front of, near, between* or *among*:

1. The dining room is ________ the kitchen and the bedroom.
2. I proudly stood ________ my two brothers.

3. The small boys played ________ their house with their father.
4. The frightened girl stood ________ her mother.
5. The drunkard stood ________ my car, so I could not drive on.
6. The tiger stood ________ the frightened man who wanted to run away.
7. The swimming pool is ________ my house, so I generally walk to the pool for a swim.
8. The watchman stood ________ the gate.
9. The teacher stood ________ the students.
10. The farmer stood ________ the trees.

EXERCISE 69

Fill in the blanks with *of, with, at* or *by*:

1. This chair is made ________ wood.
2. We write ________ a pen.
3. I live ________ my children.
4. We sat ________ the table with our sons.
5. It is 7 O'clock ________ my watch.

EXERCISE 70

Read the following sentences, and tick the correct preposition in each:

1. The student is late (for, at) school.
2. I will stay with you (by, till) 2 O'clock.
3. The road runs (by, along) the railway line.
4. I saw many people (near, by) his shop.
5. What is (in, beneath) the pile of books.
6. Do not go (in, beyond) the market.

7. Will you solve this problem (to, for) me?
8. We shall play (after, behind) dinner.
9. He went and stood (by, after) the gate.
10. Do not write (with, by) a pencil.

EXERCISE 71

Fill in the blanks with the correct prepositions:

1. The rabbit was chased ________ (by, with) the dog.
2. He distributed the chocolates ________ (among, between) the students.
3. The young lady sat ________ (beside, besides) her husband for lunch.
4. My brother was born ________ (in, at) the hospital.
5. My neighbour was found innocent ________ (of, by) the crime.
6. The driver hit the car ________ (against, on) the wall.
7. The cars were parked ________ (between, among) the two houses.
8. I went to the market ________ (to, for) buy a book.
9. The old man ran ________ (out of, away) the house.
10. He fell ________ (from, below) the bus.

A preposition can express different kinds of meanings and relationships. A good dictionary gives these.

Above:

1. The bird flew **above** the clouds.
2. The programme lasted **above** five hours.
3. The chairman is **above** the director.

Against:

1. The ladder was placed **against** the wall.
2. He acted **against** his mother's wishes.
3. The soldiers fought courageously **against** the enemy.

At:

1. We waited **at** the airport for more than two hours.
2. Most people come to the office **at** 10 a.m.
3. Oil of good quality is sold **at** a high price.

Between:

1. The function will be held **between** 9 p.m. and 10 p.m.
2. There was no misunderstanding **between** him and me.
3. This train runs **between** two important cities.
4. **Between** them the two boys made two hundred runs.

By:

1. He was standing **by** the river.
2. He leaves for office **by** 10 a.m. every day.
3. The ditch was seen **by** my sister.
4. It is 8 a.m. **by** my watch.

Of:

1. New Zealand is in the south **of** Australia.
2. This is a book **of** short stories.
3. The outer area **of** the house was very clean.
4. The club had an area **of** 200 square metres.
5. He died **of** tuberculosis.

To:

1. He gave all his money **to** the orphanage.
2. This plane goes **to** New York.
3. It is a quarter **to** ten now.
4. We have been invited **to** dinner by our neighbour.

Prepositions (Special Note)

1. **In, at:**

   In is used with the name of countries and large towns. **At** is more often used when speaking of small towns.

   E.g. He lives in America.
   He lives at Southhall.

2. **In, at, to, into:**

   In and **at** are used when speaking of things at rest. **To** and **into** are used when speaking of things in motion.

   E.g. He is **in** bed.
   He is **at** the top of his class.
   He ran **to** his mother.
   He jumped **into** the lake.

3. **On, upon:**

   On is used when speaking of things at rest. **Upon** is used when speaking of things in motion.

   E.g. I sat **on** a chair.
   The dog sprang **upon** the thief.

4. **Till, to:**

   Till is used for time, and **to** is used for place.

   E.g. I worked **till** 9 O'clock.
   We walked **to** the market.

5. **With, by:**

   With often denotes the instrument, and **by** denotes the agent.

   E.g. He killed the bear **with** his axe.
   He was stabbed **by** the mad man **with** a knife.

6. **Since, from, for:**

   Since is used before a noun or phrase denoting some point of time and is preceded by a verb in the perfect tense.

   E.g. I have eaten nothing **since** yesterday.
   He has been studying **since** morning.

   From is also used before a noun or phrase denoting some point of time but is used with the non-perfect tense.

   E.g. I played football **from** 9 a.m to 11 a.m.
   I work **from** morning till late at night.

   For is used for a period of time.

   E.g. He has been ill **for** five days.
   He has lived with me **for** ten years.

7. **Within, in:**

   In is used before a noun denoting a period of time. It means at the end of. **Within** means before the end of.

   E.g. I shall return **in** an hour.
   I shall return **within** an hour.

8. **Beside, besides:**

   Beside means at or by the side of. **Besides** means in addition to.

   E.g. The baby lay **beside** her mother.
   Besides being intelligent, he is very well behaved.

9. **Between, among:**

   Between is used when we refer to two people or two places. **Among** is used when more than two persons or things are referred to.

E.g. There is lots of love **between** the two brothers.
The people of the locality quarrelled **among** themselves.

10. **Under, Underneath:**

Under is used with persons or things. **Underneath** is used for things only.

E.g. The assistant manager works **under** the director.
The man pushed the box **underneath** the table.

EXERCISE 72

Fill in the blanks with the phrase prepositions given below:

such as, by means of, according to, for the sake of, in spite of, in place of, out of, owing to, except for, but for.

1. ________ the rules, you must get a license for your pistol before the 31st of March.
2. ________ a minor encounter, the procession passed of peacefully.
3. Four students, ________ the thirty who sat for the examination, failed.
4. Words ________ in, of, under are called prepositions.
5. ________ the petrol shortage, very few vehicles could be seen on the road.
6. ________ the injury to two of our good players, we would have won the match.
7. ________ his ill health, the principal came to school today.
8. We express our thoughts ________ our words.
9. Put one word ________ the underlined words in all the sentences given below.

10. Good parents are always ready to make sacrifices ________ their children.

EXERCISE 73

Fill in the blanks with the following words:

with, of, at, to, about, after, on, from, for

1. I am anxious ________ know about him.

2. He is good ________ nothing.

3. He is afraid ________ snakes.

4. He is worried ________ his mother.

5. He is ashamed ________ his behaviour.

6. He is sorry ________ being rude.

7. He is keen ________ help.

8. He is tired ________ studying.

9. He is pleased ________ me.

10. He is disappointed ________ hear that.

11. He is dependent ________ me.

12. He is busy ________ his work.

13. He is sensitive ________ his remarks.

14. He is well known ________ his wisdom.

15. He is qualified ________ the job.

Here is a list of some commonly used verbs and the prepositions that go with them.

1. agree to a plan, suggestion.
2. aim at a position, object.
3. apologize to someone.
4. arrive at a place, conclusion.
5. believe in something.

6. boast of something.
7. call on someone.
8. call at home.
9. call for an explanation.
10. catch up with someone.
11. complain of pain.
12. confide in someone.
13. depend on someone.
14. deprive of something.
15. guard against danger.
16. inform of something.
17. insist on something.
18. invite to lunch.
19. keep away from someone or something.
20. laugh at someone or something.
21. long for something.
22. look down upon something or someone.
23. look forward to something.
24. meddle with something.
25. object to something.
26. part from someone.
27. part with something.
28. put up with something.
29. quarrel over something.
30. recover from illness.
31. refer to a book.
32. rely on someone.
33. remind of something.
34. stand by someone.
35. search for something.

36. suspect of something.
37. sympathise with someone.
38. take revenge on someone.
39. warn against something.
40. yield to a temptation, a threat.

Here is a list of some commonly used adjectives and the prepositions that go with them.

1. abhorrent to someone.
2. addicted to a habit.
3. affectionate to someone.
4. afraid of something.
5. angry with a person.
6. ashamed of something.
7. busy with something.
8. capable of something.
9. confident of success.
10. conscious of something.
11. contented with something.
12. deficient in something.
13. disappointed with someone.
14. disgusted with someone, something.
15. disqualified for a post.
16. envious of someone.
17. famous for something.
18. favourable to someone, something.
19. fond of something.
20. gifted with an ability.
21. good at something.
22. grateful to someone.
23. guilty of a crime.

24. ignorant of something.
25. indifferent to something.
26. intimate with someone.
27. jealous of somebody, something.
28. mistaken for someone, something.
29. obliged to someone.
30. occupied with some work.
31. preferable to something.
32. proud of something.
33. satisfied with something.
34. short of something needed.
35. slow at something.
36. suitable for a purpose, occasion.
37. sure of something.
38. suspicious of someone, something.
39. tolerant of/towards somebody, something.
40. worthy of praise.

Here is a list of some commonly used combinations of noun and prepositions.

1. appetite for something (food).
2. attention to something.
3. aversion to something.
4. comparison with something.
5. concern about a matter.
6. contempt for someone, something.
7. control of something.
8. craving for something.
9. descendant of someone.
10. desire for something.
11. difference between two or more things.

12. distaste for something.
13. excuse for doing something.
14. expert in something.
15. faith in a person, belief.
16. fondness for something.
17. habit of doing something.
18. hunger for something.
19. interest in something.
20. invitation to a wedding, dinner.
21. knowledge of something.
22. love for something.
23. objection to something.
24. penalty for an offence.
25. preference for something, someone.
26. prejudice against something, someone.
27. proficiency in something.
28. proof of something.
29. provision for something.
30. punishment for a crime.
31. recovery from an illness.
32. reply to some question, letter.
33. request for something.
34. reward for something.
35. substitute for something.
36. superiority over someone.
37. taste for something.
38. thankful to someone.
39. victim of circumstances.
40. witness to a happening.

17

Conversation

Brown: Good evening, Ms Smith. This is John Brown. May I speak to Mr Smith?

Ms Smith: Certainly, Mr Brown. Hold the line please.

The Wilsons took a vacation last summer. They went to Springfield. They visited Ms Wilson's parents. They stayed there for two weeks. They had an enjoyable visit. The children liked Springfield. The Wilsons left for Springfield on Saturday morning. They got up early and dressed quickly. They ate their breakfast around eight-thirty. Then Mr Wilson drove the car to the filling station. He spoke to the attendant.

Mr Wilson: Fill it up please.

Attendant: Do you want me to check the oil?

Mr Wilson: Yes, and check the air pressure in the tyres too.

Attendant: Please move the car to the air pump.
Mr Wilson, everything is checked. You need only a quarter of oil.

Mr Wilson: Put it in. How much do I owe you?

Attendant: The gas and the oil come to twenty-seven dollars and fifty cents.

Mr Wilson returned home. The family was ready to leave. They packed the suitcase and kept them in the car. Bobby locked the windows and doors. Ms Wilson cancelled the newspaper subscription by phone. They then began the long trip to Springfield.

Q. When did the Wilsons take a trip to Springfield?

A. They took it last summer.

Q. Whom did they visit?

A. They visited Ms Wilson's parents.

Q. When did they leave?

A. They left on Saturday morning.

Q. What did they take with them?

A. They took their suitcases.

Q. How long did they stay?

A. They stayed for two weeks.

Q. Before leaving did they eat their breakfast early?

A. Yes, they did.

Q. Did Mr Wilson go to the filling station?

A. Yes, he did.

Q. Did Mr Wilson buy new tyres for the trip?

A. No, he didn't.

Q. Did they stay in Springfield for four weeks?

A. No, they didn't.

Q. Did Betsy enjoy the trip?

A. Yes, she did.

Q. When do you have your vacation?

A. In August and September.

Q. Does it last two months?

A. No, my vacation lasts three weeks. It begins in the third week of August and ends in first week of September.

The Wilsons went from Greenhill to Springfield by car. The trip was long. The weather was excellent during their trip.

It was a two hundred mile trip. They were tired and hungry at noon. They stopped for lunch and gas. Mr Wilson drove carefully. Ms Wilson looked at the scenery along the way. The children saw mountains, lakes and forests. The signs on the highway were interesting. Some signs read—curve, narrow bridge and railroad.

Q. Was it a short trip?

A. No, it wasn't.

Q. Were they tired and thirsty?

A. Yes, they were.

Q. Was the scenery beautiful?

A. Yes, it was.

Q. Was it a five hundred mile trip?

A. No, it wasn't.

Q. Was it a pleasant day?

A. Yes, it was.

Q. Were the children bored and unhappy?

A. No, they weren't.

Q. How was the trip?

A. It was a pleasant trip.

Q. How long was the trip?

A. It was two hundred miles.

Q. Who was tired and thirsty?

A. Betsy and Bobby were tired and thirsty.

Q. What was beautiful?

A. The scenery was beautiful.

Q. Where were the signs?

A. The signs were along the highway.

18

Conjunctions

Joining words are called **conjunctions.** They join words, groups of words or sentences. The words—*and, but, or, because, since, while, unless, before, when, until, if, though, that, so, either, neither, nor, although*—are joining words.

EXERCISE 74

Fill in the blanks with suitable conjunctions from the ones given below:

though, because, when, or, until, but, if, that.

1. I felt ________ I had met him somewhere.
2. The sky was blue and clear, ________ the sea was not calm.
3. I did not want to live in that hotel ________ it was very far.
4. They began to laugh ________ they saw the madman.
5. I shall get very angry ________ you disturb me.
6. She kept playing, ________ she was tired.
7. The policeman chased the young man ________ could not catch him.
8. He is four ________ five years old.
9. I cannot leave ________ the school is over.
10. I did not want to meet him ________ he was angry.

EXERCISE 75

Use *'and'* to join the following sentences:

e.g. She sat at the table. She wrote the application.
She sat at the table and wrote the application.

1. She gave me some money. She gave me some books.

   ____

2. The thief walked silently. The thief walked carefully.

   ____

3. He was brave. He was fearless.

   ____

4. Our house has a kitchen. Our house has a bedroom.

   ____

5. John jumped high. John caught the balloon.

   ____

EXERCISE 76

Join the following sentences with *'but'*:

1. Mary is intelligent. Mary is careless.

   ____

2. This room is small. This room is comfortable.

   ____

3. These coats are cheap. These coats are colourful.

   ____

4. The brothers agreed. The sisters did not.

   ____

5. The robber hit him on the head. He was not killed.

____

EXERCISE 77

Join the following sentences with *'or'*:

e.g. Would you like tea? Would you like coffee?
Would you like tea or coffee?

1. Do not jump. Leave the room.

____

2. Is she happy? Is she unhappy?

____

3. Shall we play? Shall we study?

____

4. Shall we take a taxi? Shall we go by train?

____

5. You should go just now. You will be late.

____

EXERCISE 78

Join the following sentences with *'because'*:

e.g. He has not gone. He is angry.
He has not gone because he is angry.

1. He did not come. The train was cancelled.

____

2. I cannot play outside. It is raining.

____

3. Jane has not come today. She is in the hospital.

4. The child walked to school. He had missed the bus.

5. They won the match. They had worked hard.

Read the following sentences carefully. Notice the conjunctions which have been filled in the blanks.

1. Harry and Joe were good friends sometime ago, but they seem to have quarrelled now.
2. When the nurse came to see the patient, he was awake.
3. Although he tried his best, he could not get the tickets.
4. We requested for a group photograph after the show was over.
5. Since I don't know him, I will not meet him.
6. I shall go to America if they give me enough money.
7. Unless you work hard, you cannot pass the examination.
8. While he was busy working, his mother called him.
9. That is the place where he was born.
10. The play had started before we got in.
11. As we all expected, John won the medal.
12. Though he is eighty years old, he is still very active.
13. His sister is much taller than he is.
14. Our school is neither big nor small.
15. It is neither very hot nor very cold in our country.
16. I cannot tell you today whether I'll be able to come or not.
17. Both his mother and his sister have got cars.
18. I didn't expect that my son would fail.
19. He is poor, yet he is happy.
20. Give me a pen or a pencil.

19

Conversation

How to go to the doctor's office?

Peter: The doctor's office is not far from here. It is at 2730 Oak Street. Take bus forty for Tenth Avenue.

Mr Wilson: Where is the bus stop?

Peter: It is two blocks from here.

Mr Wilson: How often do buses run on the street?

Peter: Every twenty minutes. You just missed one.

Mr Wilson: What luck! I'm going to have a long wait then.

Taking a bus

(Mr Wilson left home at one O'clock. He walked to the bus stop. He waited ten minutes for the bus. He got on the bus. He asked the bus driver some questions.)

Mr Wilson: Does this bus go to Oak Street?

Driver: I'm sorry. This route changed last week. You can transfer to a thirty-seven number bus at the corner where I turn.

Mr Wilson: Thank you, what is the fare?

Driver: Fifty cents, here is your transfer.

In the doctor's office

Mr Wilson: Good afternoon. I am Wilson. I have an appointment with the doctor.

Joan: Yes, Mr Wilson, you are a little early. Your appointment is at two O'clock. Please sit down and make yourself comfortable. The doctor will see you soon.

Mr Wilson: Thank you, I am in no hurry.

Mr Wilson took a magazine and sat down. Twenty minutes later, the nurse called his name. She took him to a little room. The doctor arrived soon and greeted Mr Wilson.

Doctor: Good afternoon, Mr Wilson. How do you feel? I understand you have a bad cold.

Mr Wilson: Yes, but I am feeling better now. This morning I felt terrible.

Doctor: You should take care of yourself. Let me take your blood pressure. I want to examine your throat too. Open your mouth and say, 'Aaa'. Oh! yes, you have a slight throat infection.

Mr Wilson: Will it go away soon?

Doctor: Yes, of course.
Are you allergic to antibiotics?

Mr Wilson: No, I'm not.

Doctor: I'm going to give you an injection.

Mr Wilson took his medicine. He was much better the next day. The family had a wonderful vacation in Springfield.

Smith: Hello, Mr Brown.

Brown: Hello, Mr Smith.

Smith: I want to invite you and Ms Brown to dinner tonight.

Brown: At your home?

Smith: Yes, at seven O'clock.

Brown: All right, we'll be there. Thank you for the invitation.

(Ms Wilson has a busy schedule. On Monday she does washing for the family. She also irons the clothes. She vacuums the rugs every Tuesday. She also mops the bathroom floor. On Wednesday she works in her garden. On Thursday she does some chores. She goes to the bank and the dry cleaner. She dusts the furniture on Friday. She goes to the grocery store every Saturday. She rests on Sunday.)

Q. Today is Friday. What is she doing now?

A. She is dusting the furniture now.

Q. What does she do every morning?

A. She washes the breakfast dishes.

Q. Does she go to the grocery store every Thursday?

A. No, she doesn't. She does her chores then.

Q. What does she do every Sunday morning?

A. She goes to the church and then she rests.

A Visit by a Neighbour

Ms Wilson usually finishes her work around three in the afternoon. Her neighbour sometimes visits her in the afternoon. They are good friends. Today is Thursday. Ms Drake comes over around three thirty.

Jane: Hello, Ann. How are you this afternoon?

Ann: Hi Jane. I am busy as usual. Sit down, let's have a cup of coffee.

Jane: All right. I have come to borrow a cup of sugar.

Ann: Are you baking something?

Jane: I'm baking a cake. I'm out of sugar. I'm too tired to go to the store, so I have come to ask you.

Ann: Here is your sugar.

Jane: Thanks. This coffee surely is good. I hear the children now. I better go home and finish my cake. See you tomorrow, Goodbye!

20

Interjections

An **interjection** is a word used merely to express some sudden or strong feeling. The word 'inter' means in and 'jection' means throw. We can say that an interjection is a word thrown in to express a sudden feeling of sadness, wonder, greeting, surprise, anger, joy, admiration.

We put an exclamation mark (!) after an interjection. An exclamation mark can also be put at the end of the sentence.

Words like hello, alas, bravo, hurrah, hush, oh, ah are used as interjections.

E.g. Bravo! Well done.
Alas! The poor lady died.
Oh! It is wonderful.
Hurrah! We have got it.

EXERCISE 79

Match the interjections in column A with the sentences in column B.

	A	B
1.	Oh!	The poor beggar died!
2.	Alas!	I have won the match.
3.	What!	It was a wonderful punch.
4.	Hush!	The sick lady is asleep.

5.	Hello!	You have done it again.
6.	Bravo!	How do you do?
7.	Hurrah!	I am sorry to hear that.

EXERCISE 80

Underline the interjections in the following sentences and put exclamation mark at the right place:

1. Bravo You have done well.

2. Hush The little child is resting.

3. Oh What a beautiful garden.

4. Hurrah My school has won.

5. Alas I could not go with him.

EXERCISE 81

Make sentences with the following interjections:

1. Good God! ______________________

2. Indeed! ______________________

3. Ah! ______________________

4. Oh! ______________________

5. Hello! ______________________

6. Alas! ______________________

7. What! ______________________

8. Hush! ______________________

9. Bravo! ______________________

10. Hurrah! ______________________

21

Words Often Confused

1. always, usually, often, sometimes, never
2. leave, depart, arrive
3. look at, listen to, watch
4. a piece of
5. anybody, nobody, anyone, no one

1. **Always, usually, sometimes** and **never** are adverbs of frequency which tell us how often an action is done.

   E.g. I usually get up at about eight.

   But sometimes I get up at seven.

   It is always cold in Antarctica.

   It is sometimes foggy in England.

   It is nearly always dry in the Sahara Desert.

   It is usually hot in India.

   It is often windy in Scotland.

   It is never snowy in Arizona.

2. People usually **leave**. Trains, buses and aeroplanes **leave** or **depart from**.

   E.g. The bus leaves New York at 2 O'clock.
   The bus departs from New York at 2 O'clock.

Children leave school after class XII.

You always leave your toys on the floor.

Arrive means come to.

E.g. Trains and aeroplanes arrive at the station or at the airport.

The train arrives in New York at 2 O'clock.

3. (i) We say looking at.

   E.g. They are looking at me.

   (ii) We are listening to.

   E.g. I'm listening to music.

   (iii) We say watching.

   E.g. I am watching a film.

4. We say:

   A piece of cake

   A carton of eggs

   A loaf of bread

   A slice of bread

   A box of matchsticks

   A tin of soup

   A packet of sweets

   A bag of flour

   A piece of cheese

   A bottle of milk

   A jar of jam

   A cup of tea/coffee

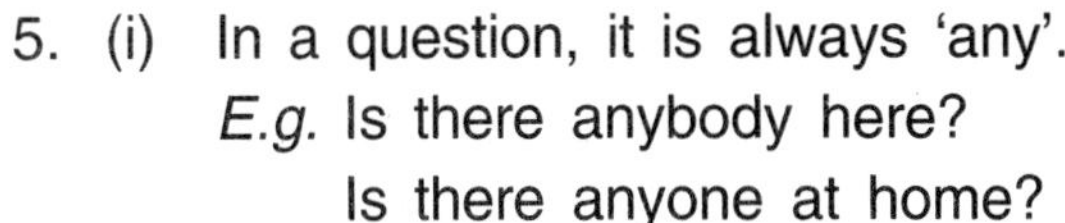

5. (i) In a question, it is always 'any'.

   E.g. Is there anybody here?

   Is there anyone at home?

(ii) In an affirmative sentence, it is always somebody or someone.

E.g. There is somebody outside.

(iii) In a negative sentences, we say:

E.g. There isn't anybody.
There isn't anyone there.
There is nobody there.
There is no one there.

(*Anybody*, *anyone* and *nobody* are all one word. *No one* is two words.)

22

Tenses

Tense means time.

There are three types of tenses:

1. Present Tense
2. Past Tense
3. Future Tense

In a sentence, it is the verb or the helping verb which decides the tense.

All the three tenses are divided into four groups.

Present Tense

1. I play cricket. (Simple Present Tense)
2. I am playing cricket. (Present Continuous Tense)
3. I have played cricket. (Present Perfect Tense)
4. I have been playing cricket. (Present Perfect Continuous Tense)

Explanation

1. **Simple Present Tense** deals with things we do generally in the present.
2. **Present Continuous Tense** deals with an action which is continuing in the present moment.
3. **Present Perfect Tense** deals with an action which has just been completed.

4. **Present Perfect Continuous Tense** deals with an action which began sometime in the past, is continuing in the present time and is likely to continue for some more time.

ASSIGNMENT

Make sentences with each of the following in all the four forms of Present Tense:

I, we, you, they, he, she, it.

Note:

I. Simple Present Tense

E.g. I play cricket.
We play cricket.
He plays cricket.
It plays cricket.
You play cricket.
She plays cricket.
They play cricket.

II. In the **Present Continuous Tense,** the helping verb **am** is used with 'I', **are** is used with plural subjects and **is** is used with third person singular number and **-ing** is used with the present form of the verb to show the continuity of action.

E.g. I am playing cricket.
We are playing cricket.
You are playing cricket.
They are playing cricket.
He is playing cricket.
She is playing cricket.
It is playing cricket.

III. In the **Present Perfect Tense, has** is used with third person singular number and **have** with other subjects. The verb is used in the past tense to show that the action has just been over.

E.g. I have played cricket.

We have played cricket.

You have played cricket.

They have played cricket.

He has played cricket.

She has played cricket.

It has played cricket.

IV. In the **Present Perfect Continuous Tense, has** is used with third person singular number and **have** with other subjects.

E.g. I have been playing cricket.

We have been playing cricket.

You have been playing cricket.

They have been playing cricket.

He has been playing cricket.

She has been playing cricket.

It has been playing cricket.

ASSIGNMENT

Using simple present tense, write down your daily routine: *e.g.*

I get up at 6 a.m. I brush my teeth and take a bath. I iron my clothes and polish my shoes. I change my clothes and eat breakfast. After that I rush to the bus stop to catch a bus. I reach office at 10 a.m. I work hard for four hours, and then I have lunch in a restaurant...

Read these sentences, and note how a change in subject brings a change in verb form.

1. Tigers **kill** goats.
   The tiger **kills** the goats.
2. The trains **stop** at big stations.
   The train **stops** at big stations.
3. They **grow** apples in the garden.
   He **grows** apples in the garden.
4. These bankers **cheat** the customers.
   This banker **cheats** the customers.
5. These magazines **give** the latest news.
   This magazine **gives** the latest news.
6. Dogs **remember** their master.
   The dog **remembers** its master.
7. Colourful curtains **make** the room bright.
   Colourful curtain **makes** the room bright.
8. Sometimes teenagers **ask** very interesting things.
   Sometimes a teenager **asks** very interesting things.
9. Birds **fly** high in the sky.
   Bird **flies** high in the sky.
10. These girls always **speak** loudly.
    This girl always **speaks** loudly.
11. We **meet** our father every month.
    He **meets** his father every month.
12. That bag **is** yellow in colour.
    Those bags **are** yellow in colour.
13. Samantha **works** for eight hours a day.
    Samantha and Joe **work** for eight hours a day.
14. She **lives** on the fourth floor of the apartment.
    We **live** on the fourth floor of the apartment.
15. They **want** to participate in the competition.
    The student **wants** to participate in the competition.

Read the -ing form of the following verbs:

1.	begin	—	beginning
2.	hit	—	hitting
3.	quarrel	—	quarrelling
4.	drink	—	drinking
5.	write	—	writing
6.	learn	—	learning
7.	read	—	reading
8.	forget	—	forgetting
9.	teach	—	teaching
10.	rise	—	rising
11.	run	—	running
12.	drink	—	drinking
13.	do	—	doing
14.	buy	—	buying
15.	come	—	coming
16.	cut	—	cutting
17.	lose	—	losing
18.	take	—	taking
19.	put	—	putting
20.	sit	—	sitting

EXERCISE 82

Solve the following puzzle with the help of the clues given. Note that all the words filled in form simple present tense of a verb.

Across

1. The eyes of cats __________ at night.
2. Many people __________ the statues of gods.
3. Rain __________ from the sky.
4. Cuckoos __________ sweetly.
5. Our mothers __________ us very well.

Down

3. Our army officers __________ bravely.
6. The sun __________ in the east.
7. An aeroplane __________ high in the sky.
8. Mary __________ her dog very hard.
9. The chairman __________ the name of every officer.
10. We __________ our office at 10 a.m.

EXERCISE 83

Write the -ing form of the following verbs:

1. read — reading
2. drive — __________
3. write — __________
4. drink — __________

5. lick — __________
6. quarrel — __________
7. hit — __________
8. buy — __________
9. hide — __________
10. sit — __________
11. put — __________
12. shut — __________

EXERCISE 84

Fill in the following blanks with the correct form of the verbs given in brackets:

1. He is ________ to God now. (pray)
2. He usually ________ to God before eating food. (pray)
3. They usually ________ the car slowly. (drive)
4. Today he is ________ the car very fast. (drive)
5. The servant is ________ on the fan now. (switch)
6. We ________ on the fan at 8 p.m. every day. (switch)
7. I ________ Pepsi, but today I am ________ Cocacola. (like, drink)
8. My mother usually ________ the newspaper in the morning. But today she is ________ something. (read, write)

EXERCISE 85

Write down the -ing form of the following verbs:

1. speak — __________
2. spread — __________
3. stitch — __________

4. skate — __________
5. open — __________
6. prepare — __________
7. beat — __________
8. eat — __________
9. spin — __________
10. slap — __________
11. cook — __________
12. play — __________

EXERCISE 86

Fill in the following blanks with the present continuous tense of the verb in brackets:

1. They _________ furniture for their new flat. (buy)
2. She _________ very fast. I am sure she will win the race. (run)
3. Tom and Mary _________ near the door. (sit)
4. I _________ up the meaning of a word in an encyclopaedia. (look)
5. You _________ your time. (utilise)
6. She _________ to her mother on the telephone. (talk)
7. It _________ heavily outside. (snow)
8. The boys _________ a loud noise. (make)
9. He _________ at the door. Please go and ask him what he wants. (knock)
10. John _________ under the car and trying to repair it. (lie)

Simple Present

1. I go to the market.

2. All the children help their friend.
3. She speaks on an interesting topic.
4. She plays the guitar.

Present Continuous

1. I am going to the market.
2. All the children are helping their friend.
3. She is speaking on an interesting topic.
4. She is playing the guitar.

Past Tense

Past Tense is also divided into four groups:

1. I played cricket. (Simple Past Tense)
2. I was playing cricket. (Past Continuous Tense)
3. I had played cricket. (Past Perfect Tense)
4. I had been playing cricket. (Past Perfect Continuous Tense)

Explanation

1. **Simple Past Tense** deals with actions of the past.
2. **Past Continuous Tense** deals with an action which was continuing at that moment in the past.
3. **Past Perfect Tense** deals with an action which had just been completed in the past.
4. **Past Perfect Continuous Tense** deals with an action which had been going for some time and would continue going on in the past for more time.

ASSIGNMENT

Make sentences with each of the following in all the four forms of past tense:

I, we, you, they, he, she, it

Note:

I. In the **Simple Past Tense**, the verb is changed into the past tense.

E.g. I played cricket. (Verb *play* changes to *played.*)

We played cricket. (Verb *play* changes to *played.*)

You played cricket. (Verb *play* changes to *played.*)

He played cricket. (Verb *play* changes to *played.*)

She played cricket. (verb *play* changes to *played.*)

It played cricket. (verb *play* changes to *played.*)

They played cricket. (verb *play* changes to *played.*)

II. In the **Past Continuous Tense**, the helping verb is changed to past tense. If the pronoun is singular, **was** is used, and if the pronoun is plural, **were** is used.

E.g. I was playing cricket.

We were playing cricket.

You were playing cricket.

He was playing cricket.

She was playing cricket.

It was playing cricket.

They were playing cricket.

III. In the **Past Perfect Tense**, the helping verb changes to *had.*

E.g. I had played cricket.

We had played cricket.

You had played cricket.

He had played cricket.

She had played cricket.

It had played cricket.

They had played cricket.

IV. In the **Past Perfect Continuous Tense**, the helping verb changes to *had been*.

E.g. I had been playing cricket.

We had been playing cricket.

You had been playing cricket.

He had been playing cricket.

She had been playing cricket.

It had been playing cricket.

They had been playing cricket.

ASSIGNMENT

Using past tense, write about what all you did yesterday.

E.g.

I got up at 6 a.m. I brushed my teeth and took a bath. I ironed my clothes and polished my shoes. I changed my clothes and ate breakfast. After that I rushed to catch a bus. I reached office at 10 a.m. I worked hard for four hours, and then I had lunch in a restaurant...

Forming the Simple Past Tense

1. walk	—	walked
2. pull	—	pulled

3. carry — carried
4. dance — danced
5. save — saved
6. creep — crept
7. learn — learnt
8. teach — taught
9. fly — flew
10. pay — paid

Read the following sentences. Drop the words in italics, and use the words given in brackets.

E.g.

1. She *usually* goes to her school at 9 a.m. (tomorrow)
   She will go to her school at 9 a.m. tomorrow.
2. We go on a holiday for *five days*. (next Monday)
   We shall go on a holiday next Monday.
3. Joe *sometimes* misses his classes. (tomorrow)
   Joe will miss his classes tomorrow.
4. I *always* go to bed at 8 O'clock. (tonight)
   I shall go to bed at 8 O'clock tonight.
5. Mr William *never* buys a new car. (next year)
   Mr William will buy a new car next year.
6. I learn my poems *every day*. (tomorrow morning)
   I shall learn my poems tomorrow morning.
7. The chairman meets the teachers on *Tuesday*. (next Wednesday)
   The chairman will meet the teachers next Wednesday.
8. We *often* play cricket. (tomorrow morning)
   We shall play cricket tomorrow morning.

Read these sentences which have been written in simple future tense.

1. If you walk in the rain, you will get wet.
2. If we miss the last train, we shall have to stay here.

3. If you reach the office late, you will get punished.
4. If Jonny stands first in the class, he will get a prize.
5. If you spend all the money, you will repent.
6. If you tease the dog, it will bite you.
7. If they reach the station late, they will miss the train.
8. If it rains very heavily, I shall come back.
9. If you run very fast, you will fall.
10. If Mary asks me, I shall tell her the truth.

EXERCISE 87

Underline the verbs in the following sentences, and write the tense of each:

1. Three cuckoos lived on a big tree. ____________
2. We shall help him. ____________
3. The princess had a magic box. ____________
4. You are right. ____________
5. We do our work every day. ____________
6. Birds lay eggs. ____________
7. The holidays will begin tomorrow. ____________
8. The queen had a dream last night. ____________
9. She was the prettiest of all. ____________
10. The soldiers are very brave. ____________
11. The intelligent man thought of a new plan. ____________
12. You will get a new dress on your birthday. ____________
13. This book costs hundred rupees. ____________
14. She tells lies. ____________

Simple present, simple past and simple future tense forms of some common verbs are given below:

Simple Present Tense

1. I break
2. You buy
3. She catches
4. They come
5. We bring
6. He calls
7. It blows
8. She chooses
9. He falls
10. He hides

Simple Past Tense

1. I broke
2. You bought
3. She caught
4. They came
5. We brought
6. He called
7. It blew
8. She chose
9. He fell
10. He hid

Simple Future Tense

1. I shall break
2. You will buy
3. She will catch
4. They will come

5. We shall bring
6. He will call
7. It will blow
8. She will choose
9. He will fall
10. He will hide

	Simple Present	Simple Past	Simple Future
1.	bite	bit	shall/will bite
2.	creep	crept	shall/will creep
3.	cut	cut	shall/will cut
4.	die	died	shall/will die
5.	do	did	shall/will do
6.	drink	drank	shall/will drink
7.	eat	ate	shall/will eat
8.	fight	fought	shall/will fight
9.	fly	flew	shall/will fly
10.	forget	forgot	shall/will forget
11.	get	got	shall/will get
12.	give	gave	shall/will give
13.	grow	grew	shall/will grow
14.	has/have	had	shall/will have
15.	hear	heard	shall/will hear
16.	jump	jumped	shall/will jump
17.	know	knew	shall/will know
18.	leave	left	shall/will leave
19.	live	lived	shall/will live
20.	look	looked	shall/will look
21.	lose	lost	shall/will lose
22.	make	made	shall/will make

23. meet	met	shall/will meet
24. open	opened	shall/will open
25. pray	prayed	shall/will pray
26. put	put	shall/will put
27. read	read	shall/will read
28. ring	rang	shall/will ring
29. rise	rose	shall/will rise
30. run	ran	shall/will run
31. say	said	shall/will say
32. see	saw	shall/will see
33. shine	shone	shall/will shine
34. sing	sang	shall/will sing
35. sleep	slept	shall/will sleep
36. speak	spoke	shall/will speak
37. stand	stood	shall/will stand
38. take	took	shall/will take
39. teach	taught	shall/will teach
40. write	wrote	shall/will write

23

Punctuation

Punctuation marks are used to make the meaning of a written piece clear to the reader. When we speak, we rely on pauses, tone, pitch and stress to make ourselves clear. When we write, we achieve this through punctuation. The most commonly used punctuation marks are:

1. Full stop (.)
2. Comma (,)
3. Question mark (?)
4. Exclamation mark (!)
5. Inverted commas (‘ ’) or (“ ”)
6. Apostrophe (’)

1. **Full stop** is used at the end of a sentence. It can also be used in abbreviations or shortened words. *E.g.*
    1. This is my son.
    2. He lives in 10 Park Street.
    3. He works for the Govt. (government)
    4. He plays football, hockey, cricket, etc. (etcetra)
    5. Co. (company), Dept. (department), e.g. (for example)
2. **Commas** separate words, phrases or clauses used within a sentence.

    The use or non-use of a comma can change the meaning of a sentence.

    Commas are used to separate words or items in a list.

Words or phrases such as however, nevertheless, for example, for instance, and that is are marked by a comma.

Commas are used to mark off question tags.

A comma is put immediately before the beginning of a quotation in direct speech.

Commas are used to separate dates and addresses. *E.g.*

1. My uncle, who retired in March, lives in Australia.
2. I would, if I were you, finish the homework just now.
3. To his surprise, she never came.
4. I bought a packet of sweets, a chocolate, one cake and two pastries.
5. You will need one register, one pencil, one sharpener and one eraser for the class.
6. "Please inform me about it," requested Tommy.
7. "Don't tell me," argued Nell, "that you have not heard about it."
8. Monday, 10th August, 1998.
9. 50 Park Avenue, 2nd Street, London.
10. You can't swim, can you?

3. **Question mark** is used after direct questions but not after indirect ones. It is used to mark the end of interrogative sentences. *E.g.*

   1. Can you tell me how?
   2. When will you come?
   3. Where are you going?
   4. How old are you?
   5. What do you have?
   6. Can you come?

7. Do you like me?
8. Does he know about it?
9. Whose watch are you wearing?
10. Who is pushing you?

4. An **exclamation mark** is put at the end of an exclamatory sentence. *E.g.*
   1. What a beautiful flower!
   2. What a bright day!
   3. Look behind you!
   4. What a big house!
   5. What a rare rose!
   6. What a sad story!
   7. Oh heavens!
   8. How stupid of him!
   9. What a question!
   10. Great piece of art!

5. **Inverted commas** or **quotation marks** are used at the beginning and at the end of direct speech. Inverted commas are also used to quote words, including titles of books, movies, etc. *E.g.*
   1. "Have you finished your lunch?" asked my cousin.
   2. Karan said, "I will cook for you."
   3. "How old are you?" asked the old man.
   4. "I will come with you," assured Jay.
   5. "Please help me," requested Ann.
   6. Have you seen 'Roman Holiday'?
   7. Have you read 'Anne Frank's Diary'?
   8. "Will you like to visit the zoo?" asked Mohan.
   9. "Don't make noise," ordered the teacher.
   10. "Get out," shouted the principal.

6. **Apostrophes** are used to indicate that some letters have been left out. *E.g.*
   1. don't (do not)
   2. It's (it is)
   3. couldn't (could not)
   4. shouldn't (should not)
   5. won't (will not)
   6. can't (can not)
   7. wouldn't (would not)
   8. aren't (are not)
   9. hadn't (had not)
   10. haven't (have not)

   Possessive pronouns do not take an apostrophe. *E.g.* yours, hers, theirs, ours, its.

   Apostrophe is also used to show possession. *E.g.*
   1. My brother's diary is in his bag.
   2. John's books are on the table.
   3. I went to Anna's school.
   4. I borrowed Rea's bicycle.
   5. Elizabeth's house is very far.

   In the case of singular noun, we use **'s**. *E.g.*
   1. The umbrella of the student
      The student's umbrella
   2. The mouth of the lion
      The lion's mouth
   3. The house of Mr William
      Mr William's house

   With plural nouns that end in **s,** we add just an apostrophe after **s.** E.g.
   1. The uniforms of the soldiers
      The soldiers' uniforms

2. The maids of the princesses
   The princesses' maids
3. The burrows of the rabbits
   The rabbits' burrows

With plural nouns that do not end in **s**, the possessive is formed by adding **'s'**. *E.g.*

1. The pencils of the children
   The children's pencils
2. The offices for men
   Men's offices
3. The bags of the women
   The women's bags

For non-living objects, we do not use an apostrophe to show possession. *E.g.*

1. We do not say—The table's legs
   We say—The legs of the table
2. We do not say—The trousers' pocket
   We say—The pocket of the trousers
3. We do not say—The pencil's colour
   We say—The colour of the pencil

ASSIGNMENT

Use an apostrophe to show possession in the following:

1. The song of the magpie
2. The scooter of my uncle
3. The bungalow of my father
4. The daughter of the industrialist
5. The lock of my mother
6. The crown of the king
7. The dress of the baby

8. The pistol of the robber
9. The gun of the king
10. The prize won by Bobby
11. The tails of the dogs
12. The frocks of the babies
13. The eyes of the cows
14. The barracks of the officers
15. The feet of the geese
16. The horns of the oxen
17. The story for children
18. The laughs of the women
19. The cars of the nurses
20. The baskets of the women

EXERCISE 88

Rewrite the following after using apostrophe:

1. The books belonging to the children

____

2. The medicine kept by the doctor

____

3. The soup meant for the kittens

____

4. The school meant for the girls

____

5. The chapel named after St. Xavier

____

EXERCISE 89

Put the apostrophe where required:

1. Its James bag. He has packed his notebooks in it.
2. It has been raining since morning.
3. Its going to snow, and Marys umbrella is in the car.
4. I did not like what he said.
5. Its not that I don't want to do it but its impossible for me to do it, cant you understand.

Read the following sentences:

1. "What is that?" mother asked Belinda in amazement.
2. "Come along young lady," he said angrily. "You are a spy who has come to steal information from me."
3. In the meantime, the Queen of Egypt and many other people saw the magnificent palace.
4. "Trees supply oxygen, so they are very important for us. Do not cut trees," demanded the forest officer.
5. "Wake up, it is six O'clock," said mother to her sleepy son.
6. "Will you go to the market today?" he asked his friend. His friend replied, "I am not going anywhere."
7. "Come with me please," pleaded my friend.
8. "The baby is asleep, may I go now?" asked the nurse.
9. "The school is closed today," the peon informed the parents.
10. "I am sorry to inform you that you have failed," said the unhappy father.

24

Address and Apostrophe

We call men **Mr**. We speak it as Mister.

Married women are **Mrs**. We speak it as Missis.

Girls and unmarried women are **Miss**. We speak it as Miss.

For both **Miss** and **Mrs**, we can use **Ms** i.e. for married and unmarried women.

APOSTROPHE

Apostrophe (') is used to show possession.

1. My uncle's pen is in his pocket.
   My uncle's pen means the pen belongs to my uncle.
2. John's books are on the table.
   John's books means the books belong to John.

In the case of singular noun, we use 's.

The seats of the passenger
The passenger's seats

The tail of the camel
The camel's tail

The house of Mr Wilson
Mr Wilson's house

With plural nouns that end in s, we add apostrophe just after s.

The guns of the soldiers
The soldiers' guns

The nests of the birds
The birds' nests

The toys of the girls.
The girls' toys

With plural nouns that do not end in s, we say—

The books of children
The children's books

The rooms for men
The men's rooms

The bags of the women
The women's bags

In case of a non-living object, we do not use an apostrophe to show possession.

We do not say:	The table's legs
We say:	The legs of the table
We do not say:	The coat's pockets
We say:	The pockets of the coat

Apostrophe is also used for contraction.

We say:

aren't	—	are not
can't	—	cannot
isn't	—	is not
doesn't	—	does not
won't	—	will not
hadn't	—	had not
shouldn't	—	should not
couldn't	—	could not
haven't	—	have not
hasn't	—	has not
I'm	—	I am

25

Homonyms, Synonyms and Antonyms

Homonyms are words that have the same pronunciation but different meanings, *e.g.*

1.	flour	flower
2.	eye	I
3.	ear	year
4.	bare	bear
5.	fete	fate
6.	hear	here
7.	there	their
8.	pair	pear
9.	gate	gait
10.	hair	hare
11.	maze	maize
12.	night	knight
13.	sale	sail
14.	buy	by
15.	see	sea
16.	for	four
17.	stare	stair

18.	are	our
19.	wear	where
20.	fair	fare
21.	weak	week
22.	wait	weight
23.	pale	pail
24.	hole	whole
25.	new	knew
26.	no	know
27.	wood	would
28.	some	sum
29.	lose	loose
30.	meet	meat
31.	dye	die
32.	hire	higher
33.	heel	heal
34.	stationary	stationery
35.	male	mail
36.	miner	minor
37.	tale	tail
38.	son	sun
39.	right	write
40.	pray	prey

Make sentences with the homonyms given above, after reading them aloud.

Read the following sentences:

1. The lady was kneading the **flour**.
   This is a fresh **flower**.
2. My **eye** is paining.
   I am a good boy.

3. My **ear** has become red.
   I will meet you after one **year**.
4. The table is **bare**.
   A big **bear** was shot yesterday.
5. He does not know his **fate**.
   A **fete** was held in our school.
6. I cannot **hear** anything.
   Please come **here** just now.
7. **There** is a school near my house.
   Their parents are coming today.
8. I bought a **pair** of trousers.
   The **pear** is a juicy fruit.
9. The **gate** of my house is made of iron.
   Her **gait** is very graceful.
10. My mother has black **hair**.
    A **hare** runs very fast.
11. She prepared **maize** soup.
    He got lost in the **maze**.
12. Stars shine at **night**.
    The **knight** fought bravely.
13. This house is for **sale**.
    The ship will **sail** tomorrow.
14. I want to **buy** a dress.
    The old man stood **by** the river.
15. I can **see** with both the eyes.
    The **sea** was very rough.
16. Wait **for** me.
    Only **four** students are sitting in the class.
17. The angry man will **stare** at the child.
    The old lady tried to climb the **stairs**.
18. They **are** coming today.
    Our school has reopened.

19. He will wear his **new** coat.
He **knew** me very well.
20. She has a **fair** complexion.
The dirver asked the passenger to pay the **fare**.
21. She is **weak** after the illness.
There are seven days in a **week**.
22. I requested my friend to **wait** for me.
I must lose **weight**.
23. She is looking very **pale**.
The boy filled the **pail** with water.
24. There is a **hole** in the bucket.
The **whole** family was happy.
25. I purchased a **new** frock.
I **knew** what he wanted.
26. I have **no** news.
I **know** his name.
27. The villagers collected **wood** from the field.
She **would** visit us soon.
28. Give me **some** money.
He solved the **sum** immediately.
29. He can **lose** his job.
The shirt is **loose** for me.
30. He will **meet** me in the cafe.
The butcher sold **meat**.
31. I told him to **dye** my shirt soon.
People **die** every day.
32. She will **hire** a house for one year.
The kite flew **higher** than we expected.
33. The child pressed his **heel** to the ground.
The wound should **heal** soon.
34. I bought six pencils from the **stationery** shop.
The child dashed into the **stationary** vehicle.

35. I received four letters in the **mail**.
    All **male** members of the family were present.
36. The **miner** looked black.
    He cannot drive because he is a **minor**.
37. She narrated a short fairy **tale**.
    A squirrel has a bushy **tail**.
38. My **son** is an army officer.
    The **sun** shines brightly.
39. I hurt my **right** hand.
    I **write** with a pencil.
40. I **pray** every day.
    The tiger leapt at its **prey**.

ASSIGNMENT

Make sentences with the following homonyms:

1. four, for
2. right, write
3. meet, meat
4. sea, see
5. here, hear

EXERCISE 90

Fill in the blanks with the correct homonyms from the brackets.

1. He is going to __________ on the blackboard. (rite, right, write)
2. The train on the station was __________. (stationary, stationery)
3. I do not know __________ the __________ will be fine enough for us to play basketball. (weather, whether)

4. You must __________ shooting in goal. (practice, practise)
5. Joe was reading the __________ issue of the magazine. (current, currant)
6. The mountaineers __________ their way when the __________ descended. (mist, missed)
7. My mother could not ______________ my jacket, __________ I had to wear it as it was. (so, sew, sow)
8. He did not care a __________ what happened (scent, sent, cent)
9. There were __________ trains going __________ New York, but both were __________ late. (to, too, two)
10. Mary passed __________ the shop but returned to __________ some oranges. (bye, buy, by)
11. The bride and the bridegroom walked down the __________ (isle, aisle)
12. It was in __________ that he tried to climb the weather __________. (vein, vain, vane)
13. It was not a suitable __________ for a hotel. (sight, cite, site)
14. __________ you mind collecting some __________ for the bonfire? (would, wood)
15. Throughout the __________ Hary looked pale and __________ after his illness. (weak, week).

ANTONYMS

An **antonym** is a word which has the opposite meaning of another. Since it must be the exact opposite of a word, it is the same part of speech. The opposite may be a different word such as fat—thin, solid—liquid, or it may be formed by adding a prefix such as comfortable—uncomfortable, loyal—disloyal, or by changing a suffix such as careful—careless, cheerful—cheerless.

ASSIGNMENT

1. Make sentences with each of the following antonyms:

1.	majority	—	minority
2.	maximum	—	minimum
3.	minor	—	major
4.	wrong	—	right
5.	vanish	—	appear
6.	convex	—	concave
7.	negative	—	positive
8.	permanent	—	temporary
9.	question	—	answer
10.	tall	—	short
11.	fat	—	thin
12.	big	—	small
13.	heavy	—	light
14.	white	—	black
15.	high	—	low
16.	young	—	old
17.	friend	—	enemy
18.	rich	—	poor
19.	crooked	—	straight
20.	light	—	dark

2. Memorise the following antonyms which have been formed by adding a prefix (before the word):

1.	complicated	—	uncomplicated
2.	certain	—	uncertain
3.	happy	—	unhappy
4.	healthy	—	unhealthy
5.	interesting	—	uninteresting

6. married — unmarried
7. kind — unkind
8. like — unlike
9. safe — unsafe
10. faithful — unfaithful
11. moral — immoral
12. order — disorder
13. perfect — imperfect
14. honour — dishonour
15. lawful — unlawful
16. thankful — unthankful
17. proper — improper
18. audible — inaudible
19. possible — impossible
20. attached — unattached
21. bearable — unbearable
22. pure — impure
23. cover — uncover
24. just — unjust
25. direct — indirect
26. stable — unstable
27. attentive — inattentive
28. ashamed — unashamed
29. partial — impartial
30. even — uneven
31. proper — improper
32. known — unknown
33. flexible — inflexible
34. capable — incapable
35. active — inactive

EXERCISE 91

Rewrite the following paragraph, by adding the prefix 'un' wherever required:

This man is married. His clothes are tidy. He is a kind man. He is walking on an even road. He is healthy and happy. He lives in a comfortable house.

____

____

____

ASSIGNMENT

Memorise the following words which have been formed by adding a suffix (after the word):

1. power — powerful
2. point — pointless
3. lazy — laziness
4. commit — commitment
5. fair — fairness
6. amaze — amazement
7. happy — happily
8. awe — awesome
9. worth — worthless
10. govern — government
11. comfort — comfortable
12. port — portable
13. child — childhood
14. excite — excitement

15. friend — friendship
16. appoint — appointment
17. good — goodness
18. favour — favourable
19. appoint — appointment
20. play — playful
21. pain — painful
22. predict — predictable
23. prefer — preferable
24. boy — boyhood
25. man — manhood
26. glad — gladly
27. fond — fondness
28. forgive — forgiveness
29. pay — payment
30. measure — measurement

SYNONYMS

A **synonym** is a word which has nearly the same meaning as another word but is slightly different. *E.g.*

1. abandon — desert, leave, quit, evacuate, jilt.
2. abbreviate — abridge, clip, compress, curtail, cut.
3. able — adept, experienced, fit, gifted, qualified.
4. abreast — alongside, beside, in touch, shoulder to shoulder, up to date with.
5. absent — away, gone, lacking, missing, out.

6. accident — calamity, casualty, chance, mishap.
7. acquire — achieve, amass, attain, buy, collect.
8. adapt — accommodate, adjust, alter, change, fit.
9. afraid — alarmed, anxious, cowardly, fearful, frightened.
10. amid — amidst, among, in the middle of, surrounded by, amongst.
11. appalling — alarming, astounding, awful, disheartening, dreadful.
12. appear — arise, arrive, develop, emerge, occur.
13. bad — defective, deficient, faulty, imperfect, incorrect, poor.
14. ban — banish, disallow, exclude, forbid, prohibit.
15. behave — act, function, operate, perform, work.
16. consume — absorb, employ, lavish, spend, use.
17. crack — break, burst, chop, snap, chip.
18. defend — cover, guard, preserve, protect, secure.
19. depression — dejection, despair, sadness, hopelessness, melancholy.
20. detain — delay, hinder, impede, retard, stop.
21. emblem — badge, crest, figure, image, mark.
22. encourage — cheer, comfort, inspire, incite, reassure.
23. energetic — active, brisk, dynamic, forceful, lively.
24. fasten — anchor, attach, bind, connect, fix, grip.

25. fatal — deadly, final, lethal, malignant, terminal.
26. fishy — doubtful, dubious, improbable, odd, queer.
27. gag — muffle, muzzle, quiet, still, suppress.
28. gallant — bold, brave, courageous, daring, fearless.
29. giddy — dizzy, faint, reeling, unsteady, frivolous.
30. giggle — cackle, chuckle, laugh, snigger, twitter.
31. hastily — fast, promptly, quickly, rapidly, speedily.
32. hazy — blurry, cloudy, dim, dull, faint.
33. health — fitness, robustness, strength, vigour, well-being.
34. impart — convey, disclose, divulge, relate, reveal.
35. impurity — adulteration, filth, foulness, pollution, admixture.
36. inaccessible — impassable, out of reach, remote, unreachable, unapproachable.
37. include — comprise, contain, cover, embrace, involve.
38. incorrect — false, faulty, improper, mistaken, inaccurate.
39. irrelevant — immaterial, inapplicable, inappropriate, unrelated, unconnected.
40. irritation — anger, annoyance, resentment, displeasure, impatience.
41. jacket — coat, covering, envelope, folder, skin, wrapper.

42. jaunty — airy, gay, lively, perky, smart.
43. join — add, annex, combine, connect, unite.
44. know — comprehend, experience, learn, notice, perceive.
45. lack — absence, deficiency, need, shortage, want.
46. lame — crippled, defective, disabled, handicapped, limping.
47. liberty — autonomy, freedom, independence, emancipation, release.
48. like — adore, love, relish, admire, appreciate.
49. madden — annoy, craze, enrage, exasperate, provoke.
50. magazine — journal, pamphlet, periodical, paper.
51. murmur — buzzling, drone, humming, mumble, muttering.
52. nasty — disgusting, horrible, foul, filthy, loathsome.
53. nimble — active, agile, alert, brisk, lively.
54. obese — fat, heavy, outsize, gross, paunchy.
55. oblige — bind, compel, constrain, make.
56. obvious — clear, distinct, evident, indisputable, inconspicuous.
57. pinnacle — crest, apex, crown, height, peak.
58. plan — design, device, idea, diagram, method.
59. quarrel — argument, brawl, discord, disagreement, dispute.
60. quick — brisk, active, fast, hasty, hurried.
61. raid — attack, seizure, assault, break into, invasion.

62. rampant — unchecked, uncontrolled, spreading like wildfire, epidemic.
63. sad — dismal, doleful, depressed, dejected, cheerless.
64. say — add, affirm, declare, mention, pronounce.
65. scar — blemish, injury, mark, wound, disfigure.
66. take — acquire, capture, catch, entrap, grasp.
67. talk — chat, chatter, communicate, gossip, speak.
68. tenacious — clinging, fast, firm, strong, tight.
69. terror — alarm, anxiety, awe, dismay, fear.
70. unappetizing — distasteful, insipid, unpleasant, uninteresting, unpalatable.
71. uncivil — bad-mannered, boorish, brusque, disrespectful, gruff.
72. vanity — airs, arrogance, conceit, egotism, frivolity.
73. venture — adventure, chance, hazard, imperil, risk, speculate, stake.
74. warm — heated, lukewarm, tepid, pleasant, cheerful.
75. wash — bathe, clean, moisten, scrub, launder.
76. yell — howl, scream, shout, shriek, cry.
77. yield — earn, generate, pay, produce, provide.
78. zest — appetite, enjoyment, gusto, flavour, interest.

26

Simple Questions and Answers

Q.1. What is your name?
Ans. My name is Joan.

Q.2. How old are you?
Ans. I am twenty years old.

Q.3. Where do you study?
Ans. I study in St. Mary's College.

Q.4. Where do you live?
Ans. I live in New York.

Q.5. What is your father's name?
Ans. My father's name is John Brown.

Q.6. What is your mother's name?
Ans. My mother's name is Mary.

Q.7. What is your brother's name?
Ans. My brother's name is William.

Q.8. What is your sister's name?
Ans. My sister's name is Vanessa.

Q.9. How many brothers do you have?
Ans. I have one brother.

Q.10. How many sisters do you have?
Ans. I have only one sister.

Q.11. What is your father's age?
Ans. My father is fifty years old.

Q.12. What is your mother's age?
Ans. My mother is forty-eight years old.

Q.13. How old is your brother?
Ans. My brother is ten years old.

Q.14. How old is your sister?
Ans. My sister is fifteen years old.

Q.15. Which is your favourite colour?
Ans. My favourite colour is blue.

Q.16. Which is your favourite game?
Ans. My favourite game is golf.

Q.17. Do you know how to swim?
Ans. Yes, I know how to swim.

Q.18. Which is your favourite fruit?
Ans. My favourite fruit is apple.

Q.19. What is the name of your teacher?
Ans. My teacher's name is Mr David.

Q.20. Which season do you like?
Ans. I like the summer season.

Q.21. Which is your favourite flower?
Ans. My favourite flower is rose.

Q.22. Which is your favourite green vegetable?
Ans. My favourite green vegetable is spinach.

Q.23. Who is your best friend?
Ans. My best friend is Anna.

Q.24. At what time do you get up?
Ans. I get up at 6 a.m.

Q.25. At what time do you sleep?
Ans. I sleep at 9 p.m.

Q.26. At what time do you go to school?
Ans. I go to school at 8 O'clock in the morning.

Q.27. Do you love your grandparents?
Ans. Yes, I love my grandparents.

Q.28. Do your grandparents love you?
Ans. Yes, my grandparents love me.

Q.29. Can you ride a bicycle?
Ans. No, I cannot ride a bicycle.

Q.30. Can you drive a car?
Ans. Yes, I can drive a car.

Q.31. When will he go home?
Ans. He will go home tomorrow.

Q.32. When will he come back?
Ans. He will come back next week.

Q.33. Who will go to the club today?
Ans. Mary and I will go to the club today.

Q.34. Will you dine in a restaurant today?
Ans. No, we will dine at home today.

Q.35. For how many hours do you play?
Ans. I play for three hours a day.

Q.36. How much money do you have?
Ans. I have very little money, only $10.

Q.37. How many magazines have you read?
Ans. I have read four magazines.

Q.38. How many articles have you written?
Ans. I have written five articles.

Q.39. How many dogs have you kept?
Ans. I have kept two dogs.

27

Use of 'Get'

1. *Get* me a glass of water.
2. He *got* me a glass of water.
3. He *had got* me a glass of water.
4. He *will get* me a glass of water.

1. *Get off* from the bus.
2. He *got off* the bus.
3. He *had got off* the bus.
4. He *will get off* the bus.

1. *Get up* early in the morning.
2. He *got up* early in the morning.
3. He *had got up* early in the morning.
4. He *will get up* early in the morning.

1. *Get down* from the stairs.
2. He *got down* from the stairs.
3. He *had got down* from the stairs.
4. He *will get down* from the stairs.

1. Please *get into* the pool.
2. He *got into* the pool.
3. He *had got into* the pool.
4. He *will get into* the pool.

1. *Get out* of my house.
2. He *got out* of my house.
3. He *had got out* of my house.
4. He *will get out* of my house.

1. *Get off* the bed.
2. He *got off* the bed.
3. He *had got off* the bed.
4. He *will get off* the bed.

1. *Get on* with your work.
2. He *got on* with his work.
3. He *had got on* with his work.
4. He *will get on* with his work.

1. *Get lost* from my room.
2. He *got lost* from my room.
3. He *had got lost* from my room.
4. He *will get lost* from my room.

1. *Get serious* with your work.
2. He *got serious* with his work.
3. He *had got serious* with his work.
4. He *will get serious* with his work.

1. *Get going* with your project.
2. He *got going* with his project.
3. He *had got going* with his project.
4. He *will get going* with his project.

1. *Get along* with your husband.
2. She *got along* with her husband.
3. She *had got along* with her husband.
4. She *will get along* with her husband.

1. *Get help* for the injured man.
2. He *got help* for the injured man.
3. He *had got help* for the injured man.
4. He *will get help* for the injured man.

1. *Get prepared* for the long journey.
2. He *got prepared* for the long journey.
3. He *had got prepared* for the long journey.
4. He *will get prepared* for the long journey.

1. *Get familiar* with that place.
2. He *got familiar* with that place.
3. He *had got familiar* with that place.
4. He *will get familiar* with that place.

1. *Get scared* of the ferocious tiger.
2. He *got scared* of the ferocious tiger.
3. He *had got scared* of the ferocious tiger.
4. He *will get scared* of the ferocious tiger.

1. *Get started* with your music lessons.
2. He *got started* with his music lessons.
3. He *had got started* with his music lessons.
4. He *will get started* with his music lessons.

1. He *gets confused* very easily.
2. He *got confused* very easily.
3. He *had got confused* very easily.
4. He *will get confused* very easily.

1. He *gets upset* with others.
2. He *got upset* with others.
3. He *had got upset* with others.
4. He *will get upset* with others.

1. *Get acquainted* with your classmates.
2. He *got acquainted* with his classmates.
3. He *had got acquainted* with his classmates.
4. He *will get acquainted* with his classmates.

1. *Get ready* to go to school.
2. He *got ready* to go to school.
3. He *had got ready* to go to school.
4. He *will get ready* to go to school.

1. I *get fed up* of him.
2. I *got fed up* of him.
3. I *had got fed up* of him.
4. I *will get fed up* of him.

1. Take medicine and *get well.*
2. He took medicine and *got well.*
3. He *had* taken medicine and *got well.*
4. He *will* take medicine and *get well.*

1. *Get information* about that leader.
2. He *got information* about that leader.
3. He *had got information* about that leader.
4. He *will get information* about that leader.

28

Do, Did, Does, Don't, Didn't, Doesn't

1. Do you like music?
   Yes, I do.
   No, I don't.
   Did you like music?
   Yes, I did.
   No, I didn't.
   Does he like music?
   Yes, he does.
   No, he doesn't.
2. Do we like music?
   Yes, we do.
   No, we don't.
   Did we like music?
   Yes, we did.
   No, we didn't.
   Does she like music?
   Yes, she does.
   No, she doesn't.
3. Do they like music?
   Yes, they do.

No, they don't.
Did they like music?
Yes, they did.
No, they didn't.
Does it like music?
Yes, it does.
No, it doesn't.

4. I do my work.
We do our work.
He does his work.
She does her work.
They do their work.
You do your work.
It does its work.

5. I don't do my work.
We don't do our work.
He doesn't do his work.
She doesn't do her work.
They don't do their work.
You don't do your work.
It doesn't do its work.

6. Don't I do my work?
Don't we do our work?
Doesn't he do his work?
Doesn't she do her work?
Don't they do their work?
Don't you do your work?
Doesn't it do its work?

7. Do I do my work?
Do we do our work?

Does he do his work?
Does she do her work?
Do they do their work?
Do you do your work?
Does it do its work?

8. Didn't I do my work?
Didn't we do our work?
Didn't he do his work?
Didn't she do her work?
Didn't they do their work?
Didn't it do its work?
Didn't you do your work?

9. I did my work.
We did our work.
He did his work.
She did her work.
They did their work.
It did its work.
You did your work.

10. I shall do my work.
We shall do our work.
He will do his work.
She will do her work.
They will do their work.
It will do its work.
You will do your work.

11. Shall I do my work?
Shall we do our work?
Will he do his work?
Will she do her work?

Will they do their work?
Will it do its work?
Will you do your work?

EXERCISE 92

Make two questions with each of the following words:

1. Do.. ?
Do.. ?

2. Did.. ?
Did.. ?

3. Does.. ?
Does.. ?

4. Don't.. ?
Don't.. ?

5. Didn't.. ?
Didn't.. ?

6. Doesn't.. ?
Doesn't.. ?

29

Who, Whose, Whom, What, Why, Which, When, Where

Que. Who is he?
Ans. He is my brother.

Que. Is he your brother?
Ans. Yes, he is. (Affirmative)
No, he isn't. (Negative)

Que. Whose book is this?
Ans. This is my book.

Que. Is this your pen?
Ans. Yes, this is. (Affirmative)
No, this isn't. (Negative)

Que. Whom did you meet?
Ans. I met my friend.

Que. Did you meet your friend?
Ans. Yes, I did. (Affirmative)
No, I didn't. (Negative)

Que. What is this?
Ans. This is a book.

Que. Is this a book?
Ans. Yes, it is. (Affirmative)
No, it isn't. (Negative)

Que. Why do you cry?
Ans. I cry because I am hurt.

Que. Are you hurt?
Ans. Yes, I am. (Affirmative)
No, I am not. (Negative)

Que. Which is your house?
Ans. This is my house.

Que. Is this your house?
Ans. Yes, this is my house. (Affirmative)
No, this is not my house. (Negative)

Que. When did you come?
Ans. I came yesterday.

Que. Did you come yesterday?
Ans. Yes, I did. (Affirmative)
No, I didn't. (Negative)

Que. Where do you live?
Ans. I live in London.

Que. Do you live in London?
Ans. Yes, I do. (Affirmative)
No, I don't. (Negative)

Que. Who are they?
Ans. They are my friends.

Que. Are they your friends?
Ans. Yes, they are. (Affirmative)
No, they aren't. (Negative)

Que. Whose books are these?
Ans. These are my books.

Que. Are these your books?
Ans. Yes, these are. (Affirmative)
No, these aren't. (Negative)

Que. Whom did they meet?
Ans. They met their friends.

Que. Did they meet their friends?
Ans. Yes, they did. (Affirmative)
No, they didn't. (Negative)

Que. What are these?
Ans. These are books.

Que. Are these books?
Ans. Yes, these are. (Affirmative)
No, these aren't. (Negative)

Que. Why did they cry?
Ans. They cried because they were hurt.

Que. Did they cry because they were hurt?
Ans. Yes, they did. (Affirmative)
No, they didn't. (Negative)

Que. Which are their houses?
Ans. These are their houses.

Que. Are these their houses?
Ans. Yes, these are. (Affirmative)
No, these aren't. (Negative)

Que. When did they come?
Ans. They came yesterday.

Que. Did they come yesterday?
Ans. Yes, they did. (Affirmative)
No, they didn't (Negative)

Que. Where do they live?
Ans. They live in London.

Que. Do they live in London?
Ans. Yes, they do. (Affirmative)
No, they don't. (Negative)

EXERCISE 93

Make questions and answers (one each) with the following words:

1. **Que.** Why ________________________________?
   Ans. ________________________________
2. **Que.** Who ________________________________?
   Ans. ________________________________
3. **Que.** Whose ________________________________?
   Ans. ________________________________
4. **Que.** Whom ________________________________?
   Ans. ________________________________
5. **Que.** What ________________________________?
   Ans. ________________________________
6. **Que.** Which ________________________________?
   Ans. ________________________________
7. **Que.** When ________________________________?
   Ans. ________________________________
8. **Que.** Where ________________________________?
   Ans. ________________________________

30

Has, Have, Had, Hasn't, Haven't, Hadn't

1. Has he come today?
   He has come today.
   He hasn't come today.
   Yes, he has.
   No, he hasn't.
2. Had he come yesterday?
   He had come yesterday.
   He hadn't come yesterday.
   Yes, he had.
   No, he hadn't.
3. Have they come today?
   They have come today.
   They haven't come today.
   Yes, they have.
   No, they haven't.
4. Had they come yesterday?
   They had come yesterday.

They hadn't come yesterday.
Yes, they had.
No, they hadn't.

5. Has she come today?
She has come today.
She hasn't come today.
Yes, she has.
No, she hasn't.

6. Had she come yesterday?
She had come yesterday.
She hadn't come yesterday.
Yes, she had.
No, she hadn't.

7. Hasn't he come today?
He hasn't come today.
He has come today.
No, he hasn't.

8. Hasn't she come today?
She hasn't come today.
She has come today.
No, she hasn't.

9. Haven't they come today?
They haven't come today.
They have come today.
No, they haven't.

10. Hadn't he come yesterday?
He hadn't come yesterday.
He had come yesterday.
No, he hadn't.

11. Hadn't she come yesterday?
    She hadn't come yesterday.
    She had come yesterday.
    No, she hadn't.

12. Hadn't they come yesterday?
    They hadn't come yesterday.
    They had come yesterday.
    No, they hadn't.

EXERCISE 94

Make questions and answers on your own with the following words:

1. **Que.** (has) ____________________?
   Ans. (has) ____________________
2. **Que.** (have) ____________________?
   Ans. (have) ____________________
3. **Que.** (had) ____________________?
   Ans. (had) ____________________
4. **Que.** (hasn't) ____________________?
   Ans. (hasn't) ____________________
5. **Que.** (haven't) ____________________?
   Ans. (haven't) ____________________
6. **Que.** (hadn't) ____________________?
   Ans. (hadn't) ____________________

31

Group Discussion

Group discussion gives an opportunity to each individual in the group to put across his point of view. To put forward your point clearly, emphatically or forcefully in a way which is accepted and appreciated by others requires knowledge on the subject and the ability to say the right thing at the right time. Listening is a very important part of group discussion. You need to listen to the point of view of others in the group. In a group discussion, you must neither be adamant about your point of view nor be upset or angry, if others don't agree with you. Remember everyone has a right to express his point of view. Be patient and smile if you can.

In day-to-day life, we land up in discussions (sometimes heated discussion) at a number of places—at home, at work, at play, at a social gathering. In fact, wherever people get together, there is a discussion on some topic or the other. To participate successfully in a discussion, one should increase one's knowledge. One should read as much as one can, and one should improve one's general awareness.

Given below are a few topics for group discussion:

1. If women go out to work, who will look after the children?
2. Men should share the household work with a smile.
3. Equal opportunities should be given to all, but there should be no reservations.

4. Dowry in a moderate form should be given to the girl.
5. Girls should have equal rights on father's property.
6. Advantages and disadvantages of living in flats.
7. Every member should share the responsibility of running a house.
8. Should children be told ghost stories?
9. Should school children take tuitions?
10. Should children be sent to a boarding school?

32

Pronunciation

Pronunciation is the way in which a word is pronounced. When we speak, it is important to pronounce the words correctly.

To improve pronunciation, you must pay attention to the following points:

1. Listen to the English news.
2. Be attentive when you hear others speak.
3. Look up the dictionary for the correct pronunciation of words.
4. Read a paragraph loudly and then tape it. After listening to the tape, correct your mistakes and speak again.
5. The formation of the mouth and placing of the tongue is important for correct pronunciation. Looking into a mirror will help.
6. Even if you go wrong sometimes, do not be discouraged.
7. Enjoy the company of people who speak fluent English.
8. Buy tapes of the speeches of great leaders of the world, and listen to them.
9. Learn the international phonetic spelling which are given below:

Phonetic Spelling

International Phonetic Alphabet (IPA)

Cut - k∧ t	Arm - a:m	her - hɜ:(r)
Sit - sɪt	See - si:	Pull - pʃ l
Too - tu:	Bed - bed	Cat - kæt
No - ɳəʃ	Saw - sɔ:	Hot - hɒt
Lunch - l∧ntʃ	Ship - ʃɪp	Jug - dʒ∧g
Pleasure - 'pleʒ∂ (r)	Yellow - 'jelə ʃ	
Thin - θɪn	This - ∂ɪs	
Sing - sɪɳ		

Diphthongs

Two vowels which slide into each other are called Diphthongs.

E.g.

ago	—	∂'g∂ʃ	=	∂ʃ	Diphthong
late	—	leɪt	=	eɪ	Diphthong
home	—	heʃ m	=	eʃ	Diphthong
five	—	faɪv	=	aɪ	Diphthong
now	—	naʃ	=	aʃ	Diphthong
join	—	dʒɔɪɳ	=	ɔɪ	Diphthong
near	—	nɪ∂(r)	=	ɪ∂	Diphthong
hair	—	he∂(r)	=	e∂	Diphthong
pure	—	pjʃ ə(r)	=	ʃ ∂	Diphthong
hat	—	hæt	=	æ	Diphthong

The above phonetic spelling will help you to find the correct pronunciation of words in the dictionary.

Keep note of the following points when you look up the dictionary:

1. (') shows the strong stress. It is in front of the part of the word that you say most strongly, *e.g.* about = ∂'baut.
2. (ˌ) shows the weak stress,
   e.g. academician — əˌkadə'mɪʃ(ə)n̩
3. (r) in brackets means that you say the sound only when the next word begins with a vowel. If the next word begins with a consonant we do not say (r).
   e.g. hair oil — he∂(γ)ɔɪl
   hair brush — he∂(r)br∧ʃ

EXERCISE 93

Look up the dictionary, and write down the phonetic spelling of the following words:

1. path — ____________
2. ten — ____________
3. cup — ____________
4. put — ____________
5. pen — ____________
6. bad — ____________
7. tea — ____________
8. did — ____________
9. chin — ____________
10. June — ____________
11. fall — ____________
12. voice — ____________

13. then — ______________

14. so — ______________

15. zoo — ______________

16. she — ______________

17. vision — ______________

18. how — ______________

19. man — ______________

20. yes — ______________

33

Idioms

In every language, there are some special words and phrases which have a particular meaing which is different from the meaning of individual words. These are called **idioms**.

Idioms do not follow the general rules of grammar. *E.g.*

1. To take over (to take charge).

   He took over the regiment from Col. S. Johnson.

2. To bear in mind (to remember)

   You must bear in mind that this is your only chance.

3. To put up with (to tolerate)

   I had to put up with ten guests in my small house.

4. To make out (to understand)

   I could not make out what he really expected.

5. To come round (to recover consciousness)

   He came round four hours after he had met with an accident.

6. To go into the matter (to examine)

   The principal asked the teacher to go into the matter immediately.

ASSIGNMENT

Make sentences with the following idioms:

1. To take over
2. To bear in mind
3. To put up with
4. To make out
5. To come round
6. To go into the matter
7. At odds
8. At arm's length
9. As a rule
10. As cold as stone

34

Proverbs

1. **A stitch in time saves nine.**

   When something goes wrong, if you rectify it or make amends immediately, you will have to spend very little time. But if you neglect it, you will have to spend a lot of time to get it in order.

2. **Birds of the same feather flock together.**

   People with similar habits, tastes, temperament, likes and dislikes make friends easily and are seen together often, just like the birds of the same type.

3. **Do unto others as you would have others to do to you.**

   Your behaviour towards other people should be the type you expect from them towards yourself.

4. **Once bitten twice shy.**

   A person who has suffered once will be very hesitant and reluctant to repeat the same action again.

5. **Laugh and the world laughs with you; cry and you cry alone.**

   When you are happy, you have many friends who want to share your joy, but unfortunately a sad and unhappy person is left alone.

6. **Barking dogs seldom bite.**

   People who talk too much or shout and get angry are

not dangerous; they do not harm anybody, just like a dog who barks but does not generally bite.

7. **Beauty lies in the eye of the beholder.**

   The appreciation of beauty differs from one individual to another. What one person finds beautiful may not necessarily be considered beautiful by another person and vice versa.

8. **Grass is greener on the other side of the hedge.**

   We generally get fascinated and enamoured by what we don't have or what we cannot have or what others have. But this feeling is true only till we get it. Just like the grass in our neighbour's lawn looks greener to us than the grass in our own lawn, though this may not be true.

9. **Cut your coat according to your cloth.**

   Your expenditure should be proportionate to your income. You must spend according to the money available, just as the size of your coat will have to be cut according to the size of cloth which is available.

10. **Don't count your chickens before they hatch.**

    Don't plan on your profits before you really receive these, because the assurity of your profit is only when you really have them in your hand.

11. **An empty mind is a devil's workshop.**

    We should keep ourselves usefully occupied and busy because if we have nothing worthwhile to do, our mind will be up to some mischief leading to destruction.

12. **Well begun is half done.**

    Any work we take on, must be done wholeheartedly, with complete dedication and interest right from the start. If we do so, the chances of completing the task successfully are well assured.

ASSIGNMENT

Write the explanation of the following proverbs:

1. United we stand, divided we fall.
2. Slow and steady wins the race.
3. All that glitters is not gold.
4. Every cloud has a silver lining.
5. A living dog is better than a dead lion.
6. Beggars can't be choosers.
7. Forewarned is forearmed.
8. Practice makes perfect.
9. Look before you leap.
10. Virtue is its own reward.

35

Reading

Reading is a good hobby. It is the best way to spend your leisure time. One who is fond of reading never gets bored. Books must always come first in a house. Books take you to the most exciting places. In those hours when children are lost in a book, you know that they are in the best of hands. They are wandering along the river banks, in jungles and in cities. Unlike television that does the imagining for them, reading fills children's mind with faces and places. They must picture for themselves. It enables them to create their own imaginary adventures, even to understand someone better, or see things differently. So dear readers, read as much as you can. I will guide you how to go about it.

Read the following story loudly:

A Naughty Lamb

If you have been to New Zealand, you will remember thousands of sheep over the hills, mountains and highways.

When you come across a flock of sheep on the road, you just stop your car and wait for them to go by. A good shepherd can tell at a glance exactly how many sheep are in a flock. There seem to be sheep everywhere as far as the eye could see. These sheep are in the charge of two shepherds and one dog. In fact, it is the dog who seems to be doing all the work, rushing this way and that, keeping his eye on every single sheep and nudging the sheep onto the side road. The good obedient sheep were all doing exactly as they were told and a thought struck me how wonderful it would be, if children would always behave like this. But suddenly I saw a small lamb turning and running back towards the highway; maybe he thought that nobody would notice if he ran away, but he was mistaken because the dog in no time headed for the lamb and turned him back towards the flock. I kept thinking how that one naughty lamb was like some children I know. The little boy who is always bothering the teacher. The naughty girl who causes a lot of trouble for her mother.

Could that naughty little lamb be you?

Write down the story in your own words.

Once upon a time in New Zealand a man who was travelling by road saw a flock of sheep. He could see many sheep, but he could not guess how many; but a good shepherd could guess the number just by a glance. One dog and two shepherds were looking after the sheep. The dog seemed to be doing more work than the shepherds. When one naughty lamb tried to run back, it was the dog who brought him back very fast. The author is reminded of those naughty children who do not listen to their parents and teachers. The author wants to know if the reader is one of those children.

ASSIGNMENT

1. Read a few other stories, and write down the summary in your own words.
2. Tape the summary with full expression, tone, modulation, stress and emphasis. Follow this at least twice a week.
3. Write down the difficult words of the stories you read, and write their phonetic spelling and meaning.
   e.g. Shepherd — 'ʃepəd — man who tends sheep.
   Stray — strei — wander, get lost.

36

Comprehension

Comprehension is the act or capability of understanding, especially a writing or speech. It is because of this fact that comprehension forms a very important part of conversation.

Read the following passage carefully. The answers for the questions that follow have been given for you:

When he woke, the water was still very high. Suddenly he saw a sight that made him jump up. A huge fish, a hundred times as big as Tom, came up the stream. It shone like silver from head to tail. Tom knew for sure that this must be the salmon, the king of all fish.

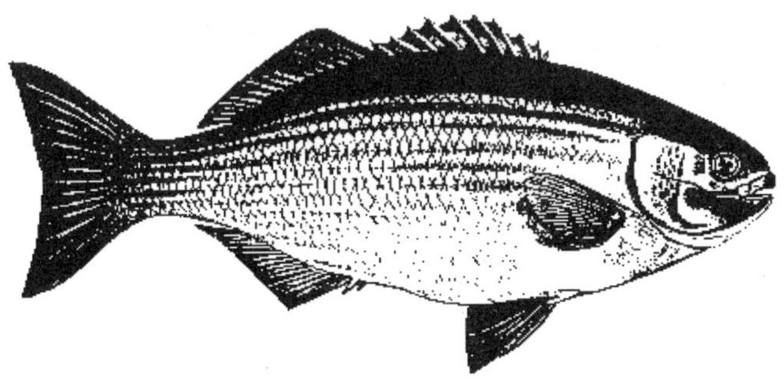

He was so frightened, he wished to creep into a hole and hide. But he need not have been, for salmons are all true gentlemen and look noble and proud. Yet, like true gentlemen, they never quarrel with anyone but mind their own business and leave rude fellows to themselves.

Q.1. Who is the main character in the paragraph?

Ans. Tom.

Q.2. Write the synonyms of the following words:

Ans. a. **proud** — conceited, arrogant.
b. **frightened** — scared, afraid.

Q.3. Write the antonyms of the following words:

Ans. a. **rude** — polite, kind.
b. **sure** — unsure, doubtful.

Q.4. What do you understand by:
a. 'the water was still very high'
b. 'a sight that made him jump up'
c. 'a hundred times as big as Tom'

Ans. a. There was a lot of water.
b. Something that frightened him.
c. Much bigger than Tom.

Q.5. Complete the present, past and past participle of the following words:

Ans. **a.** **shone** — shine, shone, shone
b. **creep** — creep, crept, crept
c. **jump** — jump, jumped, jumped
d. **woke** — wake, woke, woken
e. **quarrel** — quarrel, quarrelled, qaurrelled

Q.6. Who looks noble and proud?

Ans. The salmon looks noble and proud.

EXERCISE 96

Read the following passage carefully and answer the questions that follow:

In trying to change its direction, the leopard lost its foothold on the slippery bank and slithered into the ditch, a few feet away from Tom. Seeing this, John came dashing down the slope, swinging his axe. Others in the field had seen what was happening and a few men came running down the field with axes. They pushed John aside and made a semicircle around the snarling man-eater.

Q.1. Why was John swinging his axe?

Ans. ____________________

Q.2. Why did the leopard lose its foothold?

Ans. ____________________

Q.3. Into what did the leopard slip?

Ans. ____________________

Q.4. What had the others in the field seen?

Ans. ____________________

Q.5. What does 'dashing down' mean?

Ans. ____________________

Q.6. Write two synonyms for **snarl**.

Ans. ____________________

Q.7. Why did they make a semicircle?

Ans. ____________________

37

Telephone Conversation

Speaking on telephone is an art. Since we cannot see the person we are speaking to, it becomes very important to take extra care of our speech. The stress, modulation, warmth, emphasis—all have to be shown through the voice, since the personality of the person cannot complement it. Your conversation on telephone will differ from one person to another. You will speak differently to a well-known person, unknown person or slightly known person; your conversation will differ if you speak to an elderly person, a person of your age or a person who is younger. You must remember that your impression on the other person depends entirely and completely on your voice. So on telephone make your voice as pleasing as you can. Another point to be remembered is to be a good listener. Don't be in a great hurry to convey your point. Put across your point very politely, choose your words, be specific and to the point. If you are on a business call, make a note of all the points you want to convey, so that you don't waste any time. If you need to convey a message, write it down on a piece of paper, so that you don't forget some important points. Don't get into long discussions or arguments on the telephone. Start your telephone talk by greeting the other person and enquiring about his well-being. End your talk with a pleasant goodbye.

Read a telephone conversation between a mother and her son who is studying in a hostel and wants to come home during the summer holidays instead of going for trekking which the school has organised.

Son: Hello! Mom, How are you?

Mother: Hello, son. I am fine. Where are you speaking from?

Son: Mom, I am speaking from the hostel.

Mother: Why? What is the matter? Are you all right?

Son: Yes, Mom, I am fine. Don't worry.

Mother: Then, why have you called up?

Son: Actually Mom, I want to come home during the summer holidays.

Mother: Of course, you are coming home for a few days.

Son: Yes, but I don't want to come home for just a few days.

Mother: You are going for trekking, aren't you?

Son: Our sport's teacher is taking us out for a month for trekking and camping, but I don't want to go.

Mother: Why not?

Son: Mom, I really miss you and Dad. I want to spend more time with you.

Mother: In any case, after trekking and camping you will still be able to spend one month with us.

Son: Please! Please! Mom, I beg of you...

Mother: Son you must go with the other children for trekking because you will learn a lot.

Son: But I don't want to.

Mother: In that case, please talk to your father. I know he will not like it.

Son: OK, I'll talk to dad. When will he come back?

Mother: Around 9 p.m.

Son: OK Mom, I will call up at 9.30 p.m.

Mother: We will wait for your call.

Son: Bye, Mom! I love you!

Mother: We love you too. Bye! God bless you.

ASSIGNMENT

Write down telephone conversations on the following topics:

1. Telephone conversation between the principal and the mother of a child who has failed in the class.
2. Telephone conversation between two friends who want to go to Mumbai to attend the wedding of a common friend.
3. Telephone conversation between husband and wife when the husband informs his wife that five office friends would be coming to their house for dinner.

38

Dialogues

A **dialogue** means a talk between two people. Dialogue teaching is important to gain a command of spoken English. It trains students to express their thoughts in an easy and natural way. To prepare for a dialogue on your own, it is advisable to write the dialogue between two people. It is difficult because you have to keep in mind two imaginary persons and make them express their opposite opinions naturally and according to their characters. A spoken dialogue is spontaneous and impromptu, so an attempt should be made to avoid making it dull.

A Dialogue between a Mother and a Son

Son: Hye! Mom.

Mother: What is it?

Son: I want something from you.

Mother: What?

Son: I hope you won't say no.

Mother: Not before you tell me what it is.

Son: Give me Rs 1000/-

Mother: One thousand rupees!!!

Son: That's not too much of money.

Mother: Of course, it is. What do you want so much money for?

Son: I want to take two friends out for dinner and movie.

Mother: Why don't you suggest everyone to spend for themselves?

Son: No, Mom. I don't want to do that.

Mother: Why?

Son: I want to show off at least on one day.

Mother: Showing off is not a good habit.

Son: May not be, but one feels good.

Mother: Well! Not with your father's hard-earned money.

Son: Actually Mom my friends are poor, they cannot afford a dinner out nor can they go to a theatre.

Mother: Listen to me, my son, I have a suggestion.

Son: Yes, Mom.

Mother: It is a noble approach to think of the poor.

Son: Then have you given permission?

Mother: Listen. I suggest let your friends pay as much as they comfortably can.

Son: Why, Mom?

Mother: If they contribute what they can, they will maintain their self respect and really enjoy the evening.

Son: Will you allow me to spend the rest of the money?

Mother: One more suggestion my child. Take your friends to not so expensive eating joint and to an economical theatre.

Son: Where should we go?

Mother: Try the joint next to St. Mary's High School.

Son: That is a brilliant idea.

Mother: You must learn to cut the coat according to the cloth available.

Son: But, we have lots of money, Mom.

Mother: Yes, we do, but remember that is your father's hard-earned money. So we must spend it carefully.

Son: When I grow up and earn a lot of money, can I spend it the way I like?

Mother: Yes, but spend it wisely.

Son: How much money are you giving me?

Mother: Rs 500/-

Son: Thanks, Mom. I will return it to you when I'll start earning.

Mother: You may do so but with interest, remember.

ASSIGNMENT

Write a dialogue between a husband and a wife. The husband wants to send his daughter to a boarding school, the mother doesn't. Make use of the following words:

confidence, busy, personality, facilities, games, studies, career, goal, speech, sharing, company, lonely, homesick, weak, health, love, understanding, parents, relationship, so, many months, only, holidays, tears, letters, telephone, detached, independent, selfish, etc.

ASSIGNMENT

1. Write a dialogue between a mother and a daughter. The daughter wants to dance away through the night, mother objects.
2. Write a dialogue between a principal of a High School and the father of a boy who has failed in grade IX. 'Who is responsible for the academic performance of a child,

the school or the father?' Both feel it is the responsibility of the other.

3. Write a dialogue between father and son. The son spends a lot of money on his friends.
4. Write a dialogue between two friends on how they plan to spend the summer holidays.
5. Write a dialogue between two ladies living in a colony about their new neighbour.

39

Narrating a Story

If you are asked to tell a simple story to a child, even that requires practice and preparation. Many people tell stories badly. They repeat or omit important points which they try to squeeze in later. They drag the minor points and skip the important ones. To narrate a story, you must have the whole plot clear in your mind and the main points arranged in their proper order. Make use of dialogues in a conversation where required. Provide an interesting heading to your story. The conclusion of the story could be a bit of a surprise. The whole story should lead to the conclusion naturally.

As a preparation for narrating a story, I will give you the outline of a story. You can develop the story.

Old lady — blind — calls doctors — doctor greedy — thief — steals things — every day — treatment prolonged — nothing more to take — treatment completed — asks for fee — lady dissatisfied — the eyesight — why — cannot see the items — police — Dr. — nervous — handcuffed — prison.

STORY

Once there was an old woman who lost her eyesight all of a sudden. She was very worried and upset, so she called a doctor. The doctor checked the eyes of the old lady and assured her that her eyesight would come back within a month. The old lady was very happy and satisfied. She was waiting impatiently for the month to be over and she counted each day. On the other hand, the doctor who was very greedy, decided to trick the old lady. He started stealing a few items from her house every day. The poor old lady did not know anything because she could not see. When the doctor had removed all the items of his choice, he concentrated in curing the old lady because now he was interested in his fat fee. The old lady was improving day by day. She asked the doctor, "When will I be able to see again?" The doctor told her, "You will see the world once again on Monday." The lady waited for Monday, the day she would see light. On the appointed day, the doctor came dot on time and said, "Hello, Madam! Please sit straight on this chair, and as soon as I open the bandage, open your eyes slowly."

Old lady: I will do as you tell me.

Doctor: Can you see me?

Old lady: Yes, I can.

Doctor: (impatiently) Thank God. Now give me my fees.

Old lady: (Suspiciously looked around and noticed that most of the valuable items in her house were missing.) But I can't pay your fee because my eyesight has not been fully restored.

Doctor: How can you say that?

Old lady: I can't see many of the items which were there in the house.

The smart old lady quickly called for the police and the doctor was handcuffed and taken to prison.

After building stories from a given outline you will feel confident to narrate stories to children and your nephews and nieces at home.

ASSIGNMENT

Try building up the following story:

A miser ___ lost 100 gold coin ___ announces reward ___ 10 gold coins ___ no news ___ a poor man ___ purse 100 gold coin ___ gives the miser ___ happy ___ walks away ___ the poor man ___ surprised asks reward ___ no reward ___ 10 gold coins missing ___ so reward already take ___ poor man ___ king ___ justice ___ king ___ gives purse to poor man ___ miser surprised ___ begs to give back his money ___ king announces purse doesn't belong to miser ___ this purse only 100 gold coins ___ miser had 110 gold coins ___ miser begs for mercy ___ has to give ___ poor man ___ happy.

40

On the Spot Speaking

On the spot speaking is to speak on just anything without prior preparation. A sharp and quick mind is required to speak on a topic without preparation.

E.g. Speak on **'This pencil'**.

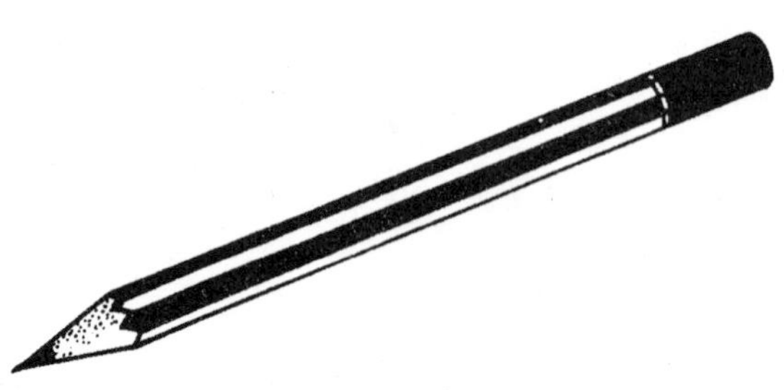

This is a pencil. It is about six inches long. It has red and blue stripes. It has been sharpened very well. This pencil belongs to me. I purchased it from a stationery shop. I paid Rs 3/- for the pencil. I keep this pencil in my bag. I am very possessive about this pencil. I do not lend my pencil to any one. I like to write with a pencil because I can erase what I write if I am not satisfied. My work is neat and clean because of this pencil. Many artists, architects, painters, writers and teachers use pencils like this one. You must also buy a pencil like this.

This rabbit

This is a rabbit. It belongs to me. It lives in a burrow with many other rabbits. It is pure white and very soft. I love its red vigilant eyes. It nibbles carrots and cabbage. When I come home, this rabbit greets me by jumping up and wants me to pet it. Many children come to play with this rabbit. This rabbit sometimes sleeps with me. I call this rabbit 'Fluff'. This rabbit runs very fast. I can never catch it.

ASSIGNMENT

Speak on the spot on the following topics:

1. My dining table
2. Loyalty
3. A friend
4. A new car
5. Poverty

To help you speak without a break, keep in mind the following points:

1. Tape what you speak. This will help you develop confidence and get rid of shyness.
2. Solve word puzzles and brain-teasers to sharpen your brain.
3. Read any and everything you can lay your hands on.
4. Play 'speaking on any topic' as a game with your friends and your family members.

5. Read any article written on a particular topic. Close the text and speak aloud what you remember.
6. Memorize a given text. Speak it aloud or tape it.
7. When you speak, there is no need to use new and difficult words. Use words which come naturally and easily to you.
8. The topic you choose should be an easy one. You should speak in a very simple language like the examples given overleaf.

41

Changing the Tense of a Story

Little Red Boat

How Jhonny loved his little red boat! It was his pride and joy. Daddy had given it to him on his birthday, and there was nothing he loved more in all the world. Sometimes he would sail it on the river that ran not far from his home. Of course, he kept a strong string tied to it, so it wouldn't float away, and he could have it again anytime he wanted to. Then one day the children who lived in the big house across the street invited Jhonny to come and play in their swimming pool and to bring his little red boat with him.

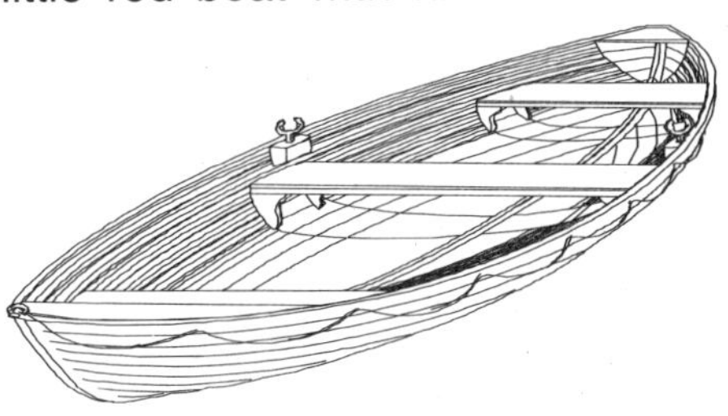

Jhonny was delighted. Picking up his boat, he said goodbye to his mother.

"Don't forget to bring it back with you," said his mother.

"I won't," said Jhonny, and he was off.

He had a great time playing in the swimming pool, but there were so many other children there that after a while he felt that his boat was in the way. So he put it in what he thought was a safe place under the kitchen window and went back to play in the pool.

When it was time to go home, Jhonny went to pick up his boat. But it wasn't there.

"Where's my boat?" he cried. "Who's taken my little red boat?"

Nobody knew. He looked all over the place, but it was nowhere to be found.

"Somebody must have taken it," he said. "I know exactly where I left it."

"Where did you leave it?" asked the lady of the house.

"Right under that window," replied Jhonny.

"Oh," said the lady. "Now I understand what has happened. You must have put your boat right next to the dustbin and when the dustbin man came this afternoon, he thought it was a part of the rubbish and took it away."

"Oh, no!" sighed Jhonny. "Not my little red boat!"

It was a heartbroken little boy who returned home that evening. Mother felt very sorry for him, as he sobbed out his story.

"I shouldn't have taken it there," he wailed. "Now most likely it's all burnt up at the city dump."

"It could be," said mother. "They usually burn everything as it arrives. But lets not give up hope too soon. Why not tell Jesus about your boat and see if he will do something. He might, you know."

So they knelt by the sofa and said a little prayer asking Jesus to look after the little boat that meant so much to Jhonny. Next morning, bright and early, mother drove Jhonny and his two sisters out to the city dump. It was a sorry looking place, with piles of rubbish everywhere, many still smouldering and smoking from the previous day's fires. Mother and the children spread out, going from one pile to another, hoping against hope that one of them would find the little red boat.

Suddenly, a happy cry rang out across the big ugly dump.

"I've got it! I've got it!" cried Jhonny.

There it was, lying barely three feet from a still burning pile. It wasn't hurt at all. Like the three Hebrews in Nebuchadnezzars' 'burning, fiery furnace', there wasn't even the smell of fire on it.

Jhonny was more thankful than you can imagine to think that Jesus cared enough to save his little red boat.

Change the tense of this story wherever possible.

How Jhonny loves his little red boat! It is his pride and joy. Daddy has given it to him on his birthday, and there is nothing he loves more in all the world. Sometimes he sails it on the river that runs not far from his house. Of course, he keeps a strong string tied to it, so it doesn't float away, and he can have it again anytime he wants to.

Then one day the children who live in the big house across the street invite Jhonny to come and play in their swimming pool and to bring his little red boat with him. Jhonny is delighted. Picking up his boat, he says goodbye to mother.

"Don't forget to bring it back with you," says mother.

"I won't," says Jhonny, and he is off. He has a great time playing in the swimming pool, but there are so many other children there that after a while he feels that his boat is in the way. So he puts it in what he thinks is a safe place under the kitchen window and goes back to play in the pool.

When it is time to go home, Jhonny goes to pick up his boat. But it isn't there.

"Where's my boat?" he cries. "Who's taken my little red boat?"

Nobody knows. He looks all over the place, but it is nowhere to be found.

"Somebody must have taken it," he says. "I know exactly where I left it."

"Where did you leave it?" asks the lady of the house.

"Right under that window," replied Jhonny.

"Oh," says the lady. "Now I understand what has happened. You must have put your boat right next to the dustbin and when the dustbin man came this afternoon, he thought it was a part of the rubbish and took it away."

"Oh, no!" sighs Jhonny. "Not my little red boat!"

It is a heartbroken boy who returns home this evening. Mother feels very sorry for him, as he sobs out his story.

"I shouldn't have taken it there," he wails. "Now most likely it's all burnt up at the city dump."

"It could be," says mother. "They usually burn everything as it arrives. But let's not give up hope too soon. Why not tell Jesus about your boat and see if he will do something. He might, you know."

So they kneel by the sofa and say a little prayer asking Jesus to look after the little boat that meant so much to Jhonny. Next morning, bright and early, mother drives Jhonny and his two sisters out to the city dump. It is a sorry looking place, with piles of rubbish everywhere, many still smouldering and smoking from the previous day's fires.

Mother and the children spread out, going from one pile to another, hoping against hope that one of them would find the little red boat. Suddenly, a happy cry rings out across the big ugly dump.

"I've got it! I've got it!" cries Jhonny. There it is, lying barely three feet from a still burning pile. It isn't hurt at all. Like the three Hebrews in Nebuchadnezzars' 'burning, fiery furnace', there isn't even the smell of fire on it. Jhonny is more thankful than you can imagine to think that Jesus cares enough to save his little red boat.

Change the story into future tense. I will begin it for you, then you can continue.

How Jhonny will love his little red boat. It will be his pride and joy. Daddy will give it to him on his birthday, and there will be nothing he will love more in all the world.

Sometimes he will sail it on the river that runs not far from his home. Of course, he will keep a strong string tied to it so, it will not float away, and he will have it again anytime he will want to.

Then one day, the children who will live in the big house across the street will invite Jhonny to come and play in their swimming pool and to bring his little red boat with him.

ASSIGNMENT

Read the above stories written in different tenses loudly and clearly. This will help you to change the tense as and when required in conversation.

42

Time, Days of the Week, Months of the Year

Time

Time forms a very important part of our daily lives. Everything revolves around time. Very often we hear this question, "What is the time?" There is a lot of explanation to be given if we are late to school or office. The exact time is what we generally want to know when we want to watch a T.V. serial, go to the theatre, meet a friend, expect guests to dinner, wait for an important phone call, catch a train or a flight, etc. It is because of these reasons I have included this chapter. In this chapter we will learn how to read and tell the time.

One day has 24 hours.
One hour has 60 minutes.
One minute has 60 seconds.

A watch shows twelve hours. It shows sixty minutes for each hour and sixty seconds for each minute. It shows three needles or hands as we call them; one to show the hour, one to show the minutes and one to show the seconds. We divide the time to a.m. and p.m. to make 24 hours, *i.e.* one day.

a.m. — ante meridiem

p.m. — post meridiem

Time can be spoken in different ways.

See the time in the clock given below!

The time given in this watch above can be read in the following ways:

1. Five minutes to twelve O'clock
2. Five to twelve
3. Eleven fifty-five

1. Quarter past twelve
2. Twelve fifteen
3. Fifteen minutes past twelve O'clock

1. A quarter to twelve
2. Fifteen minutes to twelve O'clock
3. Eleven forty-five

1. Half past twelve
2. Twelve thirty
3. Thirty minutes past twelve O'clock

1. Five past twelve
2. Twelve five
3. Five minutes past 12 O'clock

When we want to ask the time, we say:

What time is it?

What is the time?

Weather

What is the weather like?

The weather is wet.

The weather is windy.

The weather is very cold.

The weather is cloudy.

The weather is foggy.

The weather is snowy.

The weather is dry and sunny.

There are four **seasons** in the year —

spring, summer, autumn and winter.

Read these sentences aloud:

1. Anna is wearing a coat because it is cold.
2. John is wearing sunglasses because it is sunny.
3. Penny has got an umbrella because it is raining.
4. Bill and Harry are swimming because it is hot.
5. Timmy is wearing big boots because it is snowing.

Days and Months

There are seven **days** in a week—

Monday	Tuesday	Wednesday
Thursday	Friday	Saturday
Sunday		

We talk about weekdays. They are Monday, Tuesday, Wednesday, Thursday and Friday.

We talk about weekends. They are Saturday and Sunday.

What day is it today?

It is Monday.

What do you do on weekdays?

I go to office on weekdays.

What do you do on weekends?

I play golf on weekends.

There are twelve **months** in a year—

January	February	March
April	May	June
July	August	September
October	November	December

The first month is January. The second month is February. The third month is March. The fourth month is April. The fifth month is May. The sixth month is June. The seventh month is July. The eighth month is August. The ninth month is

September. The tenth month is October. The eleventh month is November. The twelfth month is December.

Ordinal Numbers

Figures	**Words**	**Figures**	**Words**
1st	first	2nd	second
3rd	third	4th	fourth
5th	fifth	6th	sixth
7th	seventh	8th	eighth
9th	ninth	10th	tenth
11th	eleventh	12th	twelfth

What is the date?

It's tenth of August.

What is the date?

It is May, the twenty-sixth.

It is twenty-sixth of May.

When is your birthday?

It is on July the seventh.

It is on seventh of July.

43

Reported Speech

Reported speech forms a very important part of English conversation. Very often we have to report the words of the speaker which can be reported in two ways:

1. Direct Speech
2. Indirect Speech

When we can quote the actual words the person spoke, we call it **direct speech**.

When we tell what the person said without quoting his exact words, we call it **indirect** or **reported speech**.

In direct speech, we use inverted commas. In reported speech, we do not use inverted commas.

When we change direct speech into indirect speech, we use the conjunction **that** before the indirect statement, *e.g.*

Direct: Anna said, "I am very hungry now."
Indirect: Anna said **that** she was very hungry then.

The pronoun *I* is changed to *she*.

The verb *am* is changed to *was*.

The adverb *now* is changed to *then*.

When the reporting or principal verb is in the past tense, all present tenses of the direct speech are changed into corresponding past tense.

(a) A simple present tense becomes simple past, *e.g.*

Direct : He said, "I am sick."

Indirect: He said that he was sick.

(b) A present continuous becomes past continuous, *e.g.*

Direct: He said, "My friend is writing letters."

Indirect: He said that his friend was writing letters.

(c) A present perfect becomes a past perfect, *e.g.*

Direct: He said, "I have passed the examination."

Indirect: He said that he had passed the examination.

The **shall** of the future tense is changed into **should** or **would**.

The **will** of the future tense is changed into **would** or **should**.

As a rule, the **simple past** in direct speech becomes the **past perfect** in indirect speech.

Direct: He said, "The dog died at night."

Indirect: He said that the dog had died at night.

(a) Words expressing nearness in time or place are generally changed into words expressing distance.

now — then
here — there
ago — before
thus — so
today — that day
tomorrow — the next day
yesterday — the day before
last night — the night before

Direct: He said, "I am delighted to be here this evening."

Indirect: He said that he was delighted to be there that evening.

(b) The change does not occur if the speech is reported during the same period or at the same place.

Direct: He says, “I am delighted to be here this evening.”

Indirect: He says that he is delighted to be here this evening.

(c) ‘This’ and ‘there’ are changed to ‘that’ and ‘those’ unless the thing which is pointed out is very near at the time of reporting.

When we report questions, we introduce the indirect speech by verbs like asked, enquired, etc. But if the question is not introduced by an interrogative word, the reporting verb is followed by whether/or, etc.

Direct: He said to me, “Where are you going?”

Indirect: He asked me where I was going.

Direct: “Where do you study?” asked the old man.

Indirect: The old man enquired where I studied.

Direct: He said to them, “Will you believe this man?”

Indirect: He asked them whether they would believe that man or not.

Direct: He said to me, “Do you want something?”

Indirect: He asked me if I wanted something.

When we report commands or requests, the indirect speech is introduced by verbs expressing request or command.

Direct: Jane said to Ann, “Go away.”

Indirect: Jane ordered Ann to go away.

Direct: He said to me, “Please wait for me till I return.”

Indirect: He requested me to wait for him till he returned.

When we report exclamation and wishes, the indirect speech is introduced by verbs expressing exclamation or wish.

Direct: John said, "How smart I am!"
Indirect: John exclaimed that he was very smart.

Direct: "God help me!" he cried. "I will never drive fast again.
Indirect: He called upon God to help him, and he resolved that he would never drive fast again.

Now read the following direct speech and indirect speech, and make note of the changes made when changing from direct to indirect speech.

Direct: He said, "I like this house."
Indirect: He said that he liked that house.

Direct: He said, "I am going to Delhi tomorrow."
Indirect: He said that he was going to Delhi the next day.

Direct: He said, "I am leaving my coat here."
Indirect: He said that he was leaving his coat there.

Direct: He says, "I am going to New York."
Indirect: He says that he is going to New York.

Direct: He said, "I will try it."
Indirect: He said that he would try it.

Direct: He said, "I'll come here again tomorrow."
Indirect: He said that he would go there again the next day.

Direct: He said, "I like this."
Indirect: He said that he liked that.

Direct: He said to me this afternoon, "I will come here in the evening."
Indirect: He told me that afternoon that he would go there in the evening.

Direct: He said, "I don't like this city."
Indirect: He said that he doesn't like that city.

Direct: He said, "My mother cooks our lunch.
Indirect: He said that his mother cooked their lunch.

Direct: The principal said, "The earth pulls objects towards its centre."

Indirect: The principal said that the earth pulls objects towards its centre.

Direct: He said, "I am leaving for Kolkata tonight."

Indirect: He said that he was leaving for Kolkata that night.

Direct: He said, "He is taking his examinations."

Indirect: He said that he was taking his examinations.

Direct: He said, "I have finished the work."

Indirect: He said that he had finished the work.

Direct: He said, "I have seen the White House."

Indirect: He said that he had seen the White House.

Direct: He said, "The people have been waiting for the actors' arrival."

Indirect: He said that the people had been waiting for the actors' arrival.

Direct: He said, "This restaurant has been giving us very good food."

Indirect: He said that that restaurant had been giving them very good food.

Direct: He said, "I saw the fire."

Indirect: He said that he had seen the fire.

Direct: They said, "We heard the news over the radio."

Indirect: They said that they had heard the news over the radio.

Direct: The boy said, "India became independent in 1947."

Indirect: The boy said that India had become independent in 1947.

Direct: He said, "When the principal arrived, everyone stood up."

Indirect: He said that when the principal arrived, everyone stood up.

Direct: He said, "I had waited for one hour for the train."
Indirect: He said that he had waited for one hour for the train.

Direct: He said, "They have already published the book."
Indirect: He said that they had already published the book.

Direct: He said, "We were watching the match."
Indirect: He said that they had been watching the match.

Direct: He said, "They had been waiting for this day."
Indirect: He said that they had been waiting for that day.

Direct: He said to the thief, "God will punish you for this."
Indirect: He told the thief that God would punish him for that.

Direct: He said to me, "I shall meet you at the airport."
Indirect: He told me that he would meet me at the airport.

Direct: He said, "I shall have finished the painting by tomorrow."
Indirect: He said that he would have finished the painting by the next day.

Direct: He said, "I can do it myself."
Indirect: He said that he could do it himself.

Direct: He said to me, "You may go."
Indirect: He told me that I might go.

Direct: He said, "We must wait for the train."
Indirect: He said that they must wait for the train.

Direct: The teacher said to the girls, "You will know your result tomorrow."
Indirect: The teacher told the girls that they would know their result the next day.

Direct: The nurse said to the patient, "I'll see you again in the evening."
Indirect: The nurse told the patient that she would see him again in the evening.

Direct: I said, "I'm fed up."
Indirect: I said that I was fed up.

ASSIGNMENT

Rewrite the following sentences using indirect speech.

1. The principal asked me, "Are you going to join the Hotel Management Course or the Engineering Course?"
2. "Do you want a notebook or a textbook?" the shopkeeper asked John.
3. Gini says, "Do your duty without worrying about the result."
4. He said to me, "I have often told you not to play with fire."
5. He wrote and said, "I am unable to come just now because I am very busy, but I will certainly start as soon as I am free.
6. The teacher promised, "If you come before school tomorrow, I will revise the lesson again."
7. She said to him, "What makes you stronger and braver than the other men?"
8. He said to me, "Wait until I come."
9. "Run away children," said their father.
10. "You have all done very badly!" remarked the principal.

44

Vocabulary

Vocabulary is a range of words known to an individual. Vocabulary plays a very important part in conversation. It helps the speaker to speak the correct words at the appropriate time.

Here are a few tips for increasing your vocabulary:

1. Read a few paragraphs from a newspaper or a magazine. Underline the difficult words, and find their meanings in the dictionary. Write these down in a notebook. Read the paragraphs once again, keeping in mind the meanings of the difficult words.

2. Read a short story, and underline all the adjectives. Then try to write the opposites of these words.

3. Write down as many words as you can, beginning with any one of the alphabet. After doing so, look up the dictionary to see what all you could have written. This exercise will sharpen your brain and increase your vocabulary.

4. Think of any two or three letters of English and write as many words as you can with it, *e.g. rec* — receive, recline, recite, etc.; *dep* — depend, depict, depot.

   Look up the dictionary for more words.

5. Whenever you hear a new word, write it down and look up the dictionary to find the exact meaning.

6. Listen to the English news on television or radio. Make note of the difficult words.
7. Use the new vocabulary in your conversation.

Read the words beginning with 'rec':

recall, recapture, recast, recede, receipt, receive, recent, receptable, reception, recess, recession, recharge, recheck, recipe, reciprocal, recirculate, recital, reck, reckon, reclaim, recline, recognition, recognize, recommend, recollect, recondition, record, recount, recover, recoup, recruit, rectangle, rectify, recur, recycle.

Read the words beginning with 'dep':

depart, department, departure, depend, dependent, depict, deplete, deplorable, deploy, deport, deposit, depot, depreciation, depress, deprive, depth, deputation, depute, deputy, depressurize, depredation, deprecate, depravity, depository, depose, depoliticize, deplume.

ASSIGNMENT

Read the following ten words beginning with 'rec' and ten words beginning with 'dep'. Write their meanings from the dictionary.

1. recall — ______________________
2. recede — ______________________
3. recent — ______________________
4. recess — ______________________
5. recycle — ______________________
6. receipt — ______________________
7. recipe — ______________________
8. recite — ______________________
9. recline — ______________________
10. receive — ______________________

1. depart — ____________________
2. depend — ____________________
3. deposit — ____________________
4. depress — ____________________
5. deprive — ____________________
6. dependent — ____________________
7. depth — ____________________
8. depict — ____________________
9. deplete — ____________________
10. departure — ____________________

ASSIGNMENT

Read aloud the names of the following flowers and look for these in a garden.

pansies, geranium, rose, lily, gladioli, marigold, orchid, lotus, tuberoses, daisies, snowdrop, bottle-brush, sunflower, dogflower, poppy, sweet peas, magnolia, zenia, tulips, bougainvillea, carnations, daffodil, forget-me-not, primrose, foxglove, jasmine, iris.

ASSIGNMENT

Find out the names of more flowers, and write them down in the space given below:

1. __________
2. __________
3. __________
4. __________
5. __________
6. __________

7. ____________
8. ____________
9. ____________
10. ____________

Parts of the Body

head, hair, forehead, eyebrows, eyelashes, eyelids, eyes, temple, ears, earlobes, nose, nostrils, cheeks, upper lip, lips, teeth, gums, tongue, neck, jaw, shoulders, elbow, arms, wrist, hand, palm, thumb, index finger, middle finger, ring finger, little finger, nails, back, waist, backbone, chest, lungs, stomach, naval, hips, legs, thigh, knee, ankle, feet, heel, big toe, small toes.

head: I have a big round head.

hair: My hair is black.

forehead: I have a broad forehead.

eyebrows: He has two busy eyebrows.

eyelashes: She has long eyelashes.

eyelids: The baby closed her eyelids because she wanted to sleep.

eyes: He has blue eyes.

temple: He had a pain in the temple of his head.

ears: We hear with our ears.

earlobes: She wore earrings on her earlobes.

nose: He has a long nose.

nostrils: We breathe through our nostrils.

cheeks: The little girl has chubby cheeks.

upper lip: The old man had a big moustache on his upper lip.

lips: She wore lipstick on her lips.

teeth: We have thirty-two teeth.

gums: His gums are bleeding.

tongue: The dog was licking his master with his tongue.

neck: He wore a scarf round his neck.

jaw: He opened his jaw wide when he yawned.

shoulders: He shrugged his shoulders since he did not know much.

elbow: She nudged her mother with her elbow.

arms: The mother held her baby in her arms.

wrist: The tennis player wore a wristband to protect his wrist.

hand: He shook hands with me.

palm: The palmist read my palm and foretold my future.

thumb: We have only two thumbs.

index finger: He pointed out with his index finger.

middle finger: The middle finger is longer than the other fingers.

ring finger: She wore a diamond ring on her ring finger.

little finger: The little finger is very small.

nails: We have nails on all our fingers.

back: He patted me on my back.

waist: He wears a belt around his waist.

backbone: Keep your backbone straight when you stand.

chest: He has a broad chest.

lungs: We take in air into our lungs.

stomach: I have just had lunch, so my stomach is full.

naval: The dancer uncovered her naval.

hips: The fat lady has big hips.

legs: We walk on our legs.

thigh: The wrestler has fat thighs.

knee: The old man got down on his knees.

ankle: This lady has fractured her ankle, so she cannot walk.

feet: He wears size ten shoes because his feet are very big.

heel: He lifted up his heels to look tall.

big toe: We have two big toes.

small toes: We have eight small toes.

Make more sentences with all the parts of the body.

Names of a few organs:

brain, nerves, veins, heart, throat, wind pipe, food pipe, intestines, liver, kidneys, gall bladder, skin.

People and Relationships

woman	man	children
husband	wife	boy
parents	baby	girl
grandparents	granddaughter	grandson
grandmother	grandfather	uncle
mother	father	aunt
cousin	sister-in-law	brother
sister	brother-in-law	husband
nephew, niece	daughter	son

ASSIGNMENT

Read aloud the following words, and use the dictionary to find out the difference in their meanings:

1. swallow	2. gulp
3. lap	4. gobble
5. slurp	6. nibble
7. munch	8. suck
9. chew	10. sip
11. bite	12. gnaw

The Internal Organs

brain, spinal cord, throat, oesophagus, muscle, lung, heart, liver, stomach, intestines, vein, artery, kidney, pancreas, bladder.

Vegetables

cauliflower, broccoli, cabbage, turnip, lettuce, ginger, spinach, beetroot, celery, corn, coriander, black beans, string beans, peas, sweet potato, asparagus, tomatoes, cucumber, pepper, potatoes, garlic, pumpkin, radishes, mushrooms, onions, carrots.

Fresh Fruits

apple, coconut, pineapple, mango, papaya, grapefruit, orange, lemon, gooseberries, blackberries, blueberries, raspberries, strawberries, cherries, plum, apricot, peach.

Dry Fruits

fig, date, prune, raisins, apricots, cashews, peanuts, walnuts, hazelnuts, almonds, chestnuts.

Meat, Poultry and Sea Food

beef, stewing meat, steak, pork, sausage, chops, spare ribs, bacon, ham, lamb, whole chicken, turkey, duck, fish, oyster, shell fish, lobster, crabs, shrimp.

Common Prepared Foods

hot dog, baked beans, potato chips, pancakes, bun, pickle, hamburger, spaghetti, meat balls, salad dressing, tossed salad, stew, pork chops, mixed vegetables, mashed potatoes, rolls, baked potatoes, steak, cookies, egg rolls, cakes, biscuits, french fry, fried chicken, pizza, jelly, bacon, toast, coffee, tea, ice cream.

Clothes

gloves, cap, shirt, trousers, windbreaker, jeans, sweater, cardigan, pullover, boots, mittens, vest, tights, jacket, hat, scarf, tie, overcoat, coat, blazer, sweat shirt, slacks, wallet, sweat pants, sneakers, shorts, belt, buckle, shopping bag, sandal, collar, dress, purse, umbrella, overalls, shoe, blouse, saree, petticoat, skirt, salwar kameez, raincoat, three piece suit, uniform, undershirt, underpants, boxer shorts, stockings, long jeans, slip, panties, briefs, brassiere, garter belt, knee socks, slippers, pyjamas, bathrobe, night gown.

Jewellery

earrings, ring, engagement ring, wedding ring, chain, necklace, string of beads, pin, bracelet, watch, watchband, cufflinks, tiepin, tie clip, clipon earrings, pierced earrings, broach.

Roads

track, highway, avenue, lane, path, passage, pavement, street, alley, aisle, footpath, corridor, pass, subway.

Answers

EXERCISE 1

1. ball 2. bag 3. cat 4. doll
5. dog 6. bed

EXERCISE 2

1. an, The 2. a, The 3. an 4. An
5. the 6. a 7. the 8. an, The
9. An 10. an, an, The

EXERCISE 3

1. thin 2. tall 3. small 4. high
5. clean 6. ugly 7. good 8. light
9. hard 10. late

EXERCISE 4

1. red 2. red 3. green 4. green
5. blue 6. blue 7. pink 8. pink
9. white 10. white

EXERCISE 5

6. 2 7. 3 8. 5 9. 10
10. 9

EXERCISE 6

1. The sun
2. A hare
3. A chemist
4. A carpenter
5. Rainbow
6. Today
7. Dog
8. Nainital
9. New delhi
10. My mother

EXERCISE 7

1. is new
2. runs fast
3. came to the stadium today
4. is good for health
5. is in the hospital
6. is blowing
7. is roaring
8. is good for crops
9. are playing
10. is flowing

EXERCISE 8

2. cooks for me
3. build nests on trees
4. have long tails
5. is hitting the ball
6. lives near my house
7. jogs every day
8. like to eat honey
9. is very strict
10. is full of guests

EXERCISE 9

1. This is a white rubber.
2. I write with a pencil.
3. This chair is very high.
4. In my garden there are many flowers.
5. I have a brown blanket.
6. The iron is on the table.
7. The dressing table is near the window.
8. There are five chairs in the room.
9. I write with a pen.
10. The baby is crying loudly.

11. It is raining heavily outside.
12. My teacher is very strict.
13. The boys are playing in the sun.
14. I want to eat ice cream.
15. I like to eat fresh vegetables.
16. The garden is full of flowers.
17. My house is small.
18. The children are playing in the park.
19. Near my house there is a cement factory.
20. The box is full of clothes.

EXERCISE 10

1. She does not have a new frock.
2. We are not friends.
3. You are not the best swimmer.
4. They were not absent today.
5. You may not have a holiday tomorrow.
6. You do not look happy.
7. All of us do not like sweets.
8. Horses do not eat grass.
9. Do not put your pencils away.
10. Do not shut the door please.
11. She does not smile at me.
12. It does not snow heavily in the mountains.
13. The sun does not shine brightly every day.
14. She does not drink too much.
15. My uncle doesn't live in London.
16. He did not sleep before me.
17. I did not meet a little school girl.
18. The dog did not run after the cow.
19. The wolf did not kill the rabbit.
20. The lion did not roar loudly.

EXERCISE 11

1. The ladies are hungry.
2. The soldiers may go.
3. The plants have been watered.
4. Board a running bus.
5. John played well.
6. I know her.
7. Give him some water.
8. The man carried a heavy load.
9. We want to leave.
10. Read this magazine.
11. You should always come alone.
12. She can solve this puzzle.
13. We go to church every day.
14. They pay for their drinks.
15. She sings well.
16. The water froze in the bucket.
17. The cow gives milk every day.
18. She went to school on her bicycle.
19. The old man shot the deer.
20. The policeman caught the thief.

EXERCISE 12

1. Interrogative
2. Assertive
3. Imperative
4. Exclamatory
5. Interrogative
6. Imperative
7. Interrogative
8. Assertive
9. Exclamatory
10. Exclamatory
11. Imperative
12. Interrogative
13. Assertive
14. Interrogative
15. Imperative
16. Assertive
17. Assertive
18. Interrogative
19. Imperative
20. Imperative

EXERCISE 15

1. wolves
2. children
3. lions
4. ships
5. keys
6. houses
7. teeth
8. shoes
9. gloves
10. flowers

EXERCISE 16

1. lions
2. pens, table
3. geese, feet
4. medals
5. horses, holiday
6. toes, foot
7. colony, mosquitoes
8. scissors, cloth
9. spectacles
10. children, school

EXERCISE 17

1. churches
2. babies
3. mouse
4. sheep
5. storey
6. oxen
7. foxes
8. tooth
9. wife
10. offices
11. fairies
12. goose
13. heroes
14. foot
15. deer
16. roofs/rooves
17. family
18. wolves
19. children
20. shelves

EXERCISE 18

1. tigers, deer
2. children, women
3. pencils, shelves
4. policemen, thieves
5. children, benches
6. ladies, pianos
7. leaders, armies
8. magicians, handkerchiefs/handkerchieves
9. lives, men
10. servants, floors

EXERCISE 19

1. Bring your knives, forks and spoons from the kitchens.
2. The tigers have eaten up the deer.
3. Will the hunters shoot those sheep?

4. Rabbits are standing near the burrows.
5. The flowers fell from the trees.
6. The mothers look after the babies.
7. The ducks swim in the ponds.
8. You have received good education from your teachers.
9. Those girls play with dolls along with those children.
10. The mice easily got into the traps.

EXERCISE 20

1. A baby sucks his thumb.
2. A lion kills a deer.
3. A rabbit eats a carrot.
4. A bear eats honey.
5. One egg is needed for the breakfast.
6. A child plays a game.
7. He can't see without his spectacles.
8. His hand is as brown as a chestnut.
9. The mountaineer climbed a hill and a valley.
10. A monkey hangs from the branch of a tree.

EXERCISE 21

1. My aunt will help all the nieces.
2. The princess rode a black mare.
3. The lioness roared in the jungle.
4. The woman came with a big bitch.
5. The hen sat on the cow.
6. The wife and the daughter worked hard.
7. The queen was killed by her sister.
8. The girl ran after the wizard.
9. The lady greeted her mother.
10. 'Madam!' he said to the patroness.

EXERCISE 22

1. actress	2. boy	3. sister	4. hen
5. dog	6. mother	7. gentleman	8. heroine
9. horse	10. wife	11. king	12. lioness
13. man	14. niece	15. prince	16. madam
17. son	18. tigress	19. uncle	20. bull
21. bee	22. emperor	23. spinster	24. widower
25. headmistress		26. nun	27. peahen
28. milkman	29. goddess	30. washerwoman	

EXERCISE 23

1. bride	2. boy, aunt
3. peahen, mare	4. brother-in-law, poet
5. host, grandmother	6. authoress, king
7. gentleman, maidservant	8. landlady
9. priestess	10. saleswoman, prince

EXERCISE 24

1. barrack	2. den	3. burrow	4. kennel
5. convent	6. zoo	7. pen	8. hive
9. stable	10. sty		

EXERCISE 25

1. rails	2. schools	3. stage	4. gardens
5. tunnel	6. chimney	7. branches	8. kitchen
9. hose	10. trees		

EXERCISE 26

1. Uncountable	2. Countable
3. Uncountable	4. Uncountable

5. Uncountable
6. Countable
7. Uncountable
8. Uncountable
9. Countable
10. Countable
11. Countable
12. Countable
13. Countable
14. Uncountable
15. Countable
16. Countable
17. Uncountable
18. Uncountable
19. Uncountable
20. Countable

EXERCISE 27

1. They, him
2. he, us
3. He, me
4. You, us, we, you
5. You, I
6. them
7. She, them
8. He, him
9. You, us
10. I, it, me

EXERCISE 28

1. They, They
2. it, him, it, He
3. She, she, her
4. She, She, She
5. She, He, her, They

EXERCISE 29

1. himself
2. myself
3. itself
4. themselves
5. itself
6. myself
7. themselves
8. herself
9. himself
10. ourselves

EXERCISE 30

1. These clothes are hers.
2. This box is hers.
3. That camel is yours.
4. These houses are yours.

5. This car is his.
6. That shop is mine.
7. This farm is theirs.
8. This ranch is his.
9. This hotel is hers
10. This computer is his.

EXERCISE 31

1. her 2. themselves 3. him
4. I 5. me 6. mine 7. himself
8. yours 9. I, him 10. her

EXERCISE 32

1. them 2. her 3. me 4. themselves
5. They, them 6. ours 7. I, you
8. she, it 9. yours 10. them

EXERCISE 33

1. What 2. Whom 3. Who 4. Where
5. Who 6. Where 7. What 8. Who
9. What 10. What 11. Who 12. Whom
13. What 14. Where 15. Whom

EXERCISE 34

1. kind 2. narrow 3. thirty-one 4. pure
5. tiny 6. black 7. wild 8. big
9. sunny 10. beautiful 11. loud 12. busy
13. rich, one 14. dangerous 15. popular

EXERCISE 35

1. small, big, new

2. bright, fresh, colourful
3. hardworking, old, sincere
4. large, new, huge
5. interesting, old, heavy

EXERCISE 36

1. floor	2. table	3. chair	4. boy
5. child	6. girl	7. story	8. insect
9. hotel	10. day		

EXERCISE 37

1. wide - narrow	2. tight - loose
3. fresh - stale	4. honest - dishonest
5. sharp - blunt	6. long - short
7. difficult - easy	8. lazy - active
9. heavy - light	10. noisy - quiet
11. rich - poor	12. wise - foolish

EXERCISE 38

1. many	2. a little	3. much	4. fewer
5. a few			

EXERCISE 39

1. heavier	2. sincere	3. foolish	4. narrowest
5. neater	6. more	7. hottest	8. worst
9. worse	10. bad		

EXERCISE 40

1. his	2. her	3. its	4. its
5. his	6. your	7. our	8. their
9. my	10. her		

EXERCISE 41

1. biggest	2. better	3. shorter	4. more
5. best	6. faster	7. biggest	8. oldest
9. more interesting		10. prettier	11. tallest
12. wiser	13. more useful		14. farther
15. highest	16. worse	17. better	18. most
19. nicer	20. fatter		

EXERCISE 42

1. shortest	2. uglier	3. finest	4. thinnest
5. least	6. more proud		7. happiest
8. older	9. worst	10. cold	

EXERCISE 43

1. is	2. am	3. are	4. are
5. are	6. are	7. is	8. is
9. are	10. is		

EXERCISE 44

2. That book is mine.
3. The plate is in the kitchen.
4. This man is young.
5. This door is very strong.
6. That orchard is full of fruits.
7. She/He is a good child.
8. I am learning English.
9. You are a nice girl.
10. He is a busy sailor.

EXERCISE 45

1. was 2. was 3. were 4. were
5. were 6. were 7. were 8. was
9. were 10. was

EXERCISE 46

1. has 2. have 3. have 4. has
5. have 6. have 7. has 8. have
9. has 10. have

EXERCISE 47

1. spends 2. was 3. play 4. teaches
5. are 6. quarrel 7. is 8. has
9. are 10. works

EXERCISE 48

1. jump 2. drain 3. push 4. doze
5. swing 6. laugh 7. knock 8. caught
9. practise 10. doubt

EXERCISE 49

1. sitting 2. standing 3. hidden 4. hanging
5. did

EXERCISE 50

1. have done 2. did 3. done
4. done 5. did 6. done 7. had done
8. did 9. has done 10. did

EXERCISE 51

1. see 2. saw 3. seen 4. see, saw
5. seen, seen 6. seen 7. saw
8. see 9. saw 10. saw

EXERCISE 52

1. May 2. can 3. Can 4. can
5. could 6. can, might 7. can
8. can 9. could 10. May

EXERCISE 53

1. shall 2. will 3. will 4. shall
5. will

EXERCISE 54

1. should 2. Should 3. Would 4. Would
5. Would 6. would 7. would 8. would
9. should 10. should

EXERCISE 55

1. might, may not 2. won't, will
3. should, shouldn't 4. can, can't
5. might not, may 6. must, mustn't
7. Need, needn't 8. dare, dare not
9. ought, oughtn't 10. must, must not

EXERCISE 56

1. soundly 2. hard 3. fast 4. softly
5. wisely 6. slowly 7. well 8. badly
9. loudly 10. sweetly

EXERCISE 57

1. outside
2. inside
3. downstairs
4. far
5. above
6. somewhere
7. everywhere
8. below
9. underneath
10. here

EXERCISE 58

1. early
2. soon
3. tomorrow
4. now
5. daily
6. afterwards
7. monthly
8. then
9. late
10. today

EXERCISE 59

1. bravely
2. late
3. always
4. never
5. early
6. yesterday
7. brightly
8. always
9. When
10. slowly

EXERCISE 60

1. badly
2. carefully
3. cowardly
4. downwards
5. backwards
6. down
7. unkindly
8. foolishly
9. late
10. far

EXERCISE 61

1. greedily
2. lazily
3. quietly
4. sincerely
5. bravely
6. soundly
7. patiently
8. happily
9. sadly
10. willingly

EXERCISE 62

1. carefully
2. fast
3. melodiously
4. soundly

5. slowly		6. well	
7. attentively		8. patiently	
9. angrily		10. sincerely	

EXERCISE 63

2. behind	3. into	4. over	5. after
6. under	7. by	8. at	9. at
10. for	11. by	12. in front of	
13. before	14. of	15. to	16. in
17. from	18. at	19. with	20. between

EXERCISE 64

1. on	2. on	3. in	4. in
5. on	6. in	7. In	8. at
9. at	10. at		

EXERCISE 65

1. into	2. in	3. out of	4. into
5. in	6. in	7. in	8. into
9. into	10. out of		

EXERCISE 66

1. on	2. over	3. under	4. under
5. under	6. over	7. below	8. above
9. on	10. under		

EXERCISE 67

1. to	2. from	3. for	4. for
5. from, to	6. for	7. from	8. to
9. for	10. for		

EXERCISE 68

1. between
2. between
3. in front of
4. behind
5. in front of
6. near
7. near
8. near
9. among
10. among

EXERCISE 69

1. of
2. with
3. with
4. at
5. by

EXERCISE 70

1. for
2. till
3. along
4. near
5. beneath
6. beyond
7. for
8. after
9. by
10. with

EXERCISE 71

1. by
2. among
3. beside
4. in
5. of
6. against
7. between
8. to
9. out of
10. from

EXERCISE 72

1. According to
2. Except for
3. out of
4. such as
5. Owing to
6. But for
7. In spite of
8. by means of
9. in place of
10. for the sake of

EXERCISE 73

1. to
2. for
3. of
4. about

5. of	6. for	7. to	8. of
9. with	10. to	11. on	12. with
13. to	14. for	15. for	

EXERCISE 74

1. that	2. but	3. because	4. when
5. if	6. though	7. but	8. or
9. until	10. because		

EXERCISE 75

1. She gave me some money and books.
2. The thief walked silently and carefully.
3. He was brave and fearless.
4. Our house has a kitchen and a bedroom.
5. John jumped high and caught the balloon.

EXERCISE 76

1. Mary is intelligent but careless.
2. This room is small but comfortable.
3. These coats are cheap but colourful.
4. The brothers agreed but the sisters didn't.
5. The robber hit him on the head, but he was not killed.

EXERCISE 77

1. Do not jump or leave the room.
2. Is she happy or unhappy?
3. Shall we play or study?
4. Shall we take a taxi or go by train?
5. You should go just now, or you will be late.

EXERCISE 78

1. He did not come because the train was cancelled.
2. I cannot play outside because it is raining.
3. Jane has not come today because she is in the hospital.
4. The child walked to school because he had missed the bus.
5. The won the match because they had worked hard.

EXERCISE 79

1. Oh! I am sorry to hear that.
2. Alas! The poor beggar died.
3. What! You have done it again.
4. Hush! The sick lady is asleep.
5. Hello! How do you do?
6. Bravo! It was a wonderful punch.
7. Hurrah! I have won the match.

EXERCISE 80

1. Bravo! 2. Hush! 3. Oh! 4. Hurrah!
5. Alas!

EXERCISE 81

1. Good God! What have you done to your hair?
2. Indeed! It is a relaxing day.
3. Ah! It hurts me.
4. Oh! Stop shouting.
5. Hello! Are you listening?
6. Alas! I could not meet him.
7. What! Has he come back again?
8. Hush! She will hear us.
9. Bravo! Your performance was wonderul.
10. Hurrah! Our school bagged all the prizes.

EXERCISE 82

Across:

1. shine 2. worship 3. falls 4. sing
5. teach

Down:

3. fight 6. rises 7. flies 8. hits
9. knows 10. reach

EXERCISE 83

2. driving 3. writing 4. drinking 5. licking
6. quarrelling 7. hitting 8. buying
9. hiding 10. sitting 11. putting 12. shutting

EXERCISE 84

1. praying 2. prays 3. drive 4. driving
5. switching 6. switch 7. like, drinking
8. reads, writing

EXERCISE 85

1. speaking 2. spreading
3. stitching 4. skating
5. opening 6. preparing
7. beating 8. eating
9. spinning 10. slapping
11. cooking 12. playing

EXERCISE 86

1. are buying 2. is running
3. are sitting 4. am looking
5. are utilising 6. is talking

7. is snowing
8. are making
9. is knocking
10. is lying

EXERCISE 87

1. lived - past
2. shall help - future
3. had - past
4. are - present
5. do - present
6. lay - present
7. will begin - future
8. had - past
9. was - past
10. are - present
11. thought - past
12. will get - future
13. costs - present
14. tells - present

EXERCISE 88

1. The children's books
2. The doctor's medicine
3. The kittens' soup
4. The girls' school
5. St. Xavier's chapel

EXERCISE 89

1. It's James bag.
2. It's been raining since morning.
3. It's, Mary's
4. didn't
5. It's, it's can't

EXERCISE 90

1. write
2. stationary
3. whether, weather
4. practise
5. current
6. missed, mist
7. sew, so
8. cent
9. two, to, too
10. by, buy

11. aisle
12. vain, vane
13. site
14. Would, wood
15. week, weak

EXERCISE 91

1. unmarried
2. untidy
3. unkind
4. uneven
5. unhealthy
6. unhappy
7. uncomfortable

EXERCISE 92

1. Do you live in Delhi?
1. Do you like your school?
2. Did you sleep well?
2. Did you hear the news?
3. Does he obey you?
3. Does she do her homework?
4. Don't you like me?
4. Don't you get tired?
5. Didn't you meet him?
5. Didn't she tell you?
6. Doesn't she swim?
6. Doesn't he love her?

EXERCISE 93

Q.1. Why are you crying?
Ans. I am crying because he hit me.

Q.2. Who has come?
Ans. My mother has come.

Q.3. Whose book is this?
Ans. This is my book.

Q.4. Whom do you like?
Ans. I like Jane.

Q.5. What do you want?
Ans. I want a chocolate.

Q.6. Which house do you live in?
Ans. I live in that big house down the street.

Q.7. When did you come?
Ans. I came yesterday.

Q.8. Where did you go?
Ans. I went to Kolkata.

EXERCISE 94

Q.1. Has he gone to school?
Ans. He has gone to school.

Q.2. Have you eaten the apple?
Ans. I have eaten the apple.

Q.3. Had he received the guests?
Ans. He had received the guests.

Q.4. Hasn't he come back?
Ans. He hasn't come back.

Q.5. Haven't you met him?
Ans. I haven't met him.

Q.6. Hadn't he shouted enough?
Ans. He hadn't shouted enough.

EXERCISE 95

1. pa:θ	2. ten	3. k ʌp	4. pʃ t
5. pen	6. bæd	7. ti:	8. dɪd
9. tʃɪɳ	10. dʒu:ɳ	11. fɔ:l	12. vɔɪs
13. ∂eɳ	13. s∂ʃ	15. ZU:	16. ʃɪ:
17. vɪʒɳ	18. haʃ	19. mæɳ	20. jes

EXERCISE 96

1. to kill the leopard
2. the bank was slippery
3. into the ditch
4. the leopard falling into a ditch and John with his axe
5. coming down fast
6. growl, angry
7. so that the leopard could not escape.